The Awakened Sai
Within You

Dr. Anita Rajani

Copyright © 2023 by Dr.Anita Rajani

All rights reserved.

This book or any portion thereof may not be reproduced or used in any manner whatsoever without the express written permission of the respective writer of the respective content except for the use of brief quotations in a book review.

The writer of the respective work holds sole responsibility for the originality of the content and The Write Order is not responsible in any way whatsoever.

Printed in India

ISBN: 978-93-5776-821-4

First Printing, 2023

The Write Order
A division of Nasadiya Technologies Private Ltd.
Koramangala, Bengaluru
Karnataka-560029

THE WRITE ORDER PUBLICATIONS.

www.thewriteorder.com

Edited by Ridham Bassi and Anagha Somanakoppa

Typeset by MAP Systems, Bengaluru

Book Cover designed by Keerthipriya

Publishing Consultant - Deeksha

Contents

Preface xi

Foreword xii

Chapter 1: Faith - The Ultimate Path 1

Chapter 2: Be A Lotus–Padma 3

Chapter 3: The Dark Night Of The Soul 5

Chapter 4: Astrology Charts Fail, When
I Surrender To Sai 7

Chapter 5: Reading Sai Satcharitra Will Dissolve
Your Karma 9

Chapter 6: Dissolve Your Ego 11

Chapter 7: Service To Sadguru Sai Baba 13

Chapter 8: Dhuni–The Eternal Flame 15

Chapter 9: Test Of Time 17

Chapter 10: When My Desire To Live Has Ceased 19

Chapter 11: When All Is Well In My World 21

Chapter 12: My Never-Ending Problems 23

Chapter 13: When Your Wishes Are Not Granted 25

Chapter 14: Shed The Ignorance 27

Chapter 15: Sai Is My Savior 29

Chapter 16: The Act Of True Surrender 31

Chapter 17: Sai Baba's Jholi 35

Chapter 18: When Sai Baba Tests Your Patience 39

Chapter 19: What Should I Pray For? 41

Chapter 20: Why Do Good People Suffer? 43

Chapter 21: Tyrant Family Members 45

Chapter 22 : What Happens When We Curse? 47

Chapter 23: When You Take Others
Karma On Yourself 49

Chapter 24: There Are No Shortcuts In Life 51

Chapter 25: The Samadhi Grants Boon 53

Chapter 26: The Gurusthan Initiates Into
My Kingdom 57

Chapter 27: Man Proposes, God Disposes 61

Chapter 28: The Act Of Offering Food To Sai Baba ... 63

Chapter 29: The Sharanagati (Surrender) To Sai Baba 67

Chapter 30: You Are Never Alone When You Belong
To Sai Baba 69

Chapter 31: The Path Of Bhakti To Baba 71

Chapter 32: Listening To Sai's Arti 75

Chapter 33: Align Your Will With The Will Of Sai 77

Chapter 34: When We Put Dakshina In Sai Temple 79

Chapter 35: Lessons That Are Not Learnt 81

Chapter 36: Good People Die Early 83

Chapter 37: Manifestation Vs. Surrender 85

Chapter 38: Jaako Raakhe Saiyaan, Maar Sake Na Koi! 87

Chapter 39: You Must Cross The Bridge Of Pain
To Find Love 89

Chapter 40: Life Is Enriched With Gratitude 91

Chapter 41: This Too Shall Pass 93

Chapter 42: Forgive Yourself And Others 95

Chapter 43: Fear Vs. Faith 97

Chapter 44: No One Loves Me 99

Chapter 45: The Path Of Truth And Honesty 101

Chapter 46: Ascend To Merge With Sai 103

Chapter 47: Bhiksha 105

Chapter 48: Always See Humor In Your Challenges 109

Chapter 49: Karma With Words 111

Chapter 50: Baba's Promise To Mankind! 113

Prologue 117

Preface

Sai Baba: A divine light, vibrating at a high frequency, envelops all His children in His rings of Light. He manifests Himself in human form, revealing His presence to us from time to time. As the human mind has the ability to forget, He shows us that He exists in each one of us, in you and me. He is omnipotent and omnipresent, the Sadguru who enlightens us and will never abandon us. Through this book, He once again conveys His love for His children and serves as a reminder that He exists as a guiding force in all our lives.

In this book, He communicates with His children and sends His light to free us from the misconceptions, pain, and anger that our limited minds hold toward our Sadguru. He attempts to show us how our minds are limited, while His love is expansive and unconditional, embracing each one of His children within His heart and guiding each one onto His path.

This channeled book is authored by Dr. Anita Rajani, prompted by Baba Himself to write it. It seeks to clarify the doubts and questions we have about our lives and our relationship with Sai Baba. It's an ode to his life, which is a guide in itself.

This book will enlighten you and dispel the small doubts that may linger as a disciple. It answers many questions that hinder complete faith in Sai Baba. Surrender must be wholehearted for Sai Baba's miracles to manifest in your life. I hope you find joy in reading this book and experience inner healing, rising in consciousness to unite with Sai Baba. Allow each petal of your inner divine lotus to unfurl, becoming a fully bloomed one.

Om Sai Ram

Foreword

Dr. Anita has beautifully captured the key messages from our Sadguru, Shri Sainath Maharaj, in this book.

Many of us are led to believe that devotees living close to Baba during His lifetime were always happy and never experienced dark nights of the soul, as mentioned in the book. However, it's essential to note that even beloved devotees like Nana Sahib Chandorkar, whom Baba cherished deeply, had their share of hardships. Nana Sahib's daughter, Mina Tai, lost her husband at a young age, and during her pregnancy, she also lost her baby.

Mahalsapthi, Baba's closest devotee who used to sleep alongside Him, faced financial difficulties to the extent that there were times when his family didn't have enough money for food. It may seem surprising that such challenges existed while living in the presence of Parabrahma, whose blessings are abundant (I'd like to remind readers that Baba is believed to be a reincarnation of Datta Guru, as mentioned in Sri Pad Vallabh Charitra, written a hundred years ago).

These instances are not isolated, as there are many stories of devotees who approached Baba during various life-altering events. However, Baba's message remained consistent: have faith in Him and practice Saburi.

One of the most profound examples of unwavering faith is exemplified by Shyama, who, when bitten by a snake, did not seek help elsewhere but asked the villagers to take him to Dwarkamai because of his unwavering faith in Baba. Dada Saheb Khaparde himself witnessed hearing Sai Naam Samaran from Shyama's breath when he was asleep.

This level of faith and devotion, as highlighted in this book, requires going through life's ups and downs, where Baba strengthens your faith rather than testing it.

Om Sai Ram

Remember, not all blossoms turn into fruit; some may fall, while others become ripe. You must decide which path you choose to follow. This book will guide you toward the latter.

Puneet Malik is a Sai devotee who strives to share Baba's divine stories as recounted by families who lived with Him during His lifetime. You can find more of these stories on the YouTube channel below.

श्री अनंतकोटी ब्रम्हांडनायक राजाधिराज योगिराज परब्रम्ह
श्री सच्चिदानंद सद्गुरु श्री साईनाथ महाराज की जय...!

Shri Anantakoti Brahmandanayak Rajadhiraj Yogiraj Parabrahma
Shree Sachinanand Sadguru Sainath Maharaj ki Jai!!

Om Sai Ram

!! OM SAI RAM !!

Sai, in you I merge,
Sai, from you I emerge,
Hold me forever, Sai,
Be in me forever, Sai,
I belong to you, Sai,
Merge me back into you.
Om Sai Ram!!

Dr. Anita Rajani

Sai raham nazar karnaa, Bachon kaa paalan karnaa,
Sai raham nazar karnaa, Bachon kaa paalan karnaa.

Jaanaa tum neh jagat pasaaraa, Sab hee jhoott jamaanaa,
Jaanaa tum neh jagat pasaaraa, Sab hee jhoott jamaanaa,
Sai raham…

Main andhaa hoon bandaa aapkaa, Mujhse prabhu dikhlaanaa,
Main andhaa hoon bandaa aapkaa, Mujhse prabhu dikhlaanaa,
Sai raham…

Daas Ganu kahe ab kyaa bolu, Thak gayi meree rasnaa.
Daas Ganu kahe ab kyaa bolu, Thak gayi meree rasnaa.
Sai raham…

Composed by: Sri Dasganu Maharaj

English Translation:
Sai, look at us mercifully and take care of your children.
Sai, look at us mercifully and take care of your children.

You know this mundane world, this world full of illusion.
You know this mundane world, this world full of illusion.
Sai!

I am a blind and ignorant devotee of yours, give me God's vision.
I am a blind and ignorant devotee of yours, give me God's vision.
Sai!

Das Ganu says: What shall I say now? My tongue fails me.
Das Ganu says: What shall I say now? My tongue fails me.
Sai…

Chapter 1

Faith - The Ultimate Path

As humans, we tend to oscillate from our lower self to our higher self until we merge both into one. The journey of the soul is to evolve and ascend to a higher level of vibration. Every time you make a move to climb that step higher, you are pulled down by the lower energies, which create obstacles in your path towards growth. During this complete stage of evolution, A Sadguru-A Bearer of Light — is required to take you across the hurdles thrown at you. Negativity will manifest in your mind, creating negative thoughts and taking you in a downward spiral. Our Beloved Sai Baba helps to cross any negativity that comes up to stop you from rising by holding your hand across the traverse path of life.

As every human operates from the multi-level of consciousness, the karmic layers often manifest as anger at your beloved Sai; you get angry at your Guru and stop praying. You feel you have prayed, fasted, chanted Sai's name all day, visited his temples, and read the Sai Satcharitra, but what has Sai done for you? He has abandoned you during your tough times. You may feel Sai loves his other devotees and doesn't love you. You may even stop believing he exists.

You become a rebellious child, creating havoc in your own life. In this anger, you begin to self-sabotage your own success and growth. Getting angry at Sai won't help you in any way. In fact, you need him more now than ever. The rebel child needs to awaken to the larger truth of being the beloved child of Sai Baba. Then every experience becomes his Prasadam.

Sai Baba encompasses your energies and holds your space to heal and raise your faith quotient.

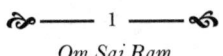

Om Sai Ram

Sai says, "My child, I am forever standing by your side—good or bad. Just as a mother never hurts her child back, no matter how much the child hurts her, I will always stand by your side unconditionally. Many times, when things are not going right in your life, you will feel like I have deserted you. That is not true! In fact, it is you who has blocked your senses due to stress, anger, hurt, and worry. That's the reason you are unable to see me. My dear child, I am carrying you in my arms and taking away 80% of the storms of your life, that comes your way onto me. I am taking all the brunt of your pain on myself. What you are facing is just 20% of your karmic storm that has surfaced for a release. Be assured that I hold you firm. I hold you in a way that you will not get hurt. In fact, you must show more faith in me at such times. Instead of stopping all the prayers, you must increase the quotient of what and how you pray. It will help you gain results faster. My dear child, I do not desert you; you push me out of your life. You need to develop more Shraddha and Saburi, the two golden words that can take you far ahead in your journey of crossing all the hurdles in your life. Your Sai Maa will never desert you. Your Sai Maa loves you forever."

Your Beloved,
Sai Baba

Prasadam - Sacred Food

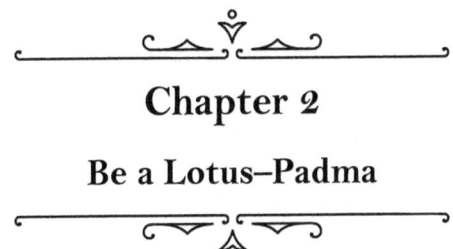

Chapter 2

Be a Lotus–Padma

The lotus is a very pure, high vibratory flower that breeds in the muck. It emerges untouched by the same muck it grows in. It has learnt the art of detachment from its external surroundings, which is why it is a flower most revered by the gods. It has passed all the tests in the realm of Earth and now deserves enough to be presented at the feet of the Lord. The humans also need to learn a lesson from the lotus- to evolve detached from the samskaras (conditioning), beliefs, vices (greed, anger, lust, addictions), attachments (people, material objects), desires (kama-lust, aishwarya-luxuries) and emerge to the true essence of their higher self, which shines so bright that it becomes a lighthouse for others to search for their own light.

One of the most beautiful ways to emerge is to do Naam Jaap (name chanting), which is taking Sai's name in your every breath and using it as a tool to clear your karmas and samskaras. Sai is Brahma, Vishnu, and Mahesh merged into one–Sai Baba. He has shown us the accurate way to live a life of detachment. He has lived the life of a Fakir-simplified life, detached from all materialistic objects, religion, name, etc. He was a pure soul on the realm of Earth.

It's so easy to be lost in the woods and waste your precious life in distractions rather than awakening to the Sai within you. Taking his name is a subconscious reminder of the path you must walk, and not a detour. When his name resonates in every cell of you, it will enlighten your soul to merge with his eternal light. When chanted, the name of Sai draws all the darkness from your mind and clears your mind of the shadows you have been carrying for many lifetimes.

Om Sai Ram

Sai says, "My dear child, the simplest form of ascension and releasing karmic debts is to take my name. My name is Sarvbrahman, Sarvavyapi. It contains the power to erase all your past karma and attain Moksha (ascension). This period Earth is a transitory period where the souls have come at this time to fasten the speed of the release of past karmas and emerge as Light. Chant my name, and you will not only clear your karma but also merge in me and the ultimate Supreme Light. My name will keep you safe from all dangers and attacks and shield you from all possible evils. Make sure you devote a few minutes daily to chanting my name. Sit in a silent space and keep chanting Sai, Sai, Sai. See my name entering the core of your being, purifying you from your innermost depth. Slowly, increase the time you spend chanting, and my name shall take you across this illusionary world and keep you safe while you cross and reach me. Your ultimate goal in life must be only to purify your soul and merge with me. Each act of yours is noted, and karma is created. The thoughts slowly have to reduce, and your mind must only be filled with light. The soul has to purify the past baggage, and an attempt must be made through a disciplined daily life of prayers and Naam Jaap. Purging is essential for the soul to feed on the nourishing energies I send you daily. Communicate with me as I am your father, mother, guide, and friend. You will never need another friend once you connect with me thoroughly. I am waiting with eagerness and open arms to embrace you."

Your Beloved,
Sai Baba

Sarvabrahman - Entire Universe
Sarvavyapi - omnipresent

Chapter 3

The Dark Night Of The Soul

Every soul on Earth at some point goes through something called the "Dark Night Of The Soul"— it's the darkest phase of a human life when one touches rock bottom, and from here, there is no way but to go up. It's easy said than done, as there is no stability of mind, the mind feels a dark shadow is cast over them from which they cannot overcome. Some experience this more than once in their lifetime, at different stages of their lives. The trials and tribulations overwhelms you, and it gets very tedious to pass this stage. At times such as these, Sadguru holds you through these trials in his strength and protects you by becoming your armor around you.

When everything starts falling apart and destruction seems inevitable, it's only the Light of the Sadguru that acts as a torch in the darkness. There is a lot of shedding of false masks that you hold through will no longer hide the truth from being exposed and help you rise like a Phoenix from the ashes. By holding Sai's hand, you can touch your true essence in real terms. This phase is so tough that you will be lost if you do not operate from conscious awareness and imbibe the qualities of Shraddha and Saburi.

The eyes will see the larger truth, and you will be in the Sharan of Sai till all passes by. The diamond goes through various tough processes to finally shine like a diamond and become precious. Similarly, life lessons are processes that help you shine like a star. The longer the dark night, the tougher the process, and the tighter Sai holds your hand and helps you across. You will feel him closer, as you will need just that to traverse across the choppy seas.

Sai says, *"I am here with you in this birth to help you shed your ego masks, to break your subtle ego, and to rise towards the light. Being with me is not an easy journey. Don't think that I will gift, only happiness. I may also send hardships and tests. My Leelas will create illusions around you, which will require you to have an eye of faith in me to break free. My tests will be your trials, which you will have to pass as it's necessary to evolve from this human mind to the Divine mind-your intellect that you are so proud of, needs to go and be replaced only and only by me – the Divine intellect. I will do all that is possible to help you rise and will never leave you alone in the darkness. This process of transformation is tough, but it is at times created by me, and it will not keep you stranded. It may seem like a dark endless tunnel, but it's all an illusion. Your problems are here to serve you. I will guide you through the process, sending you the message all the time, but you will need to have faith in me, and eyes open to pick up the messages and decode them. I will send people to you, to hold you through this process if need be, who may at times be strangers, but they will feel like your own tribe. Your duty is to keep the faith and know that I am holding your back, come what may. All my Leelas are to awaken you to your higher consciousness. I will never leave you alone and that's my promise to you, my dear child. Your Sai always keeps the promises. I follow you everywhere just the way you stay focused on me. My duty is to guide you and I do just that."*

Your Beloved,
Sai Baba

Shraddha - Faith
Saburi - Patience
Sharan - Refuge
Leelas - Divine Play/Game Of Illusions

Chapter 4

Astrology Charts Fail, When I Surrender To Sai

Life is full of challenges, hurdles, anxieties, frustrations, depression, and confusions. If you are not directed properly, you might feel lost. At times like this, you might run from pillar to post, seeking and searching for answers, and directions from various astrologers, clairvoyants, psychics, healers, and readers asking and hoping for relief from your issues. You may want to understand your next course of action. Many times, you might fall in trap with some wrong person or fall into an addictive behavior of becoming dependent on these readings and in turn, you might be feeding your fears and anxieties which can make things worse for you. You are not supposed to be looking out for quick fix solutions.

There is a reason why you are facing certain challenges: maybe to make you stronger, learn more patience, learn certain deeper lessons, break unhealthy patterns, clear some karmic debts with people, or fulfill certain soul contracts. If, instead of following your soul path, you land up running from pillar to post trying to just fix things from outside, you will leave the karmic cycle incomplete. You might be leaving karma incomplete with certain people who are just mirroring your shadow parts, your hidden subconscious patterns.

It's good to seek guidance once in a while. Sometimes you are led to them by Sai himself to serve you a message, but you need to know where to draw a line. All the answers lie within you, and only when you are aligned in an empowered way with Sai, can you decipher the messages that Sai sends you. If you have faith in Sai then your soul's blueprint changes and the charts are not relevant anymore. Your soul is now ready for spiritual transformation with the aid and guidance of Sai.

Om Sai Ram

Sai says, *"When you learn to have total faith in me, only then can you believe that when I hold the reins of your life in my hands nothing can harm you. When you realize that I stand by your side always, you will not operate from fear and anxiety. You will stand tall (steadfast) in your faith in me. No astrology chart will be valid once your soul truly surrenders to me! Your soul belongs to me! I change your blueprints and what you were born with will become null and void. If you truly believe in my existence in your life, even in tough times you will hold your center and become aware that the churning is needed to separate the poison from the elixir. It is just the Samudra manthan (inner churning) of your life process. And I ride your consciousness through it all. Only then will your life truly transform and nothing can really harm you or touch you. Instead of asking Baba why me, ask Baba how do I get across this, Believe only and only in me and see how I take you across this lifetime. Trust and believe in me only!! Your Sai is your remedy and your solution. Once you are under my Sharan. I shall erase your unnecessary diversions so that your life will smoothen out and you can do more service for the highest good of your land. I shall ensure your soul path is clear. Your soul needs to be empowered enough so as not to deter in tough times. You will see miracles after miracles. Life will become different and so will your perception to view situations, people and experiences. Have one pointed focus and you shall attain moksha."*

Your Beloved,
Sai Baba

Samudra Manthan- Inner Churning
Sharan - Refuge
Moksha - Liberation

Om Sai Ram

Chapter 5

Reading Sai Satcharitra Will Dissolve Your Karma

Sai Baba insists that each of his children must read the Sai Satcharitra. Sai explains that reading his stories will not only release you from karmic debts, but they will also free you from samskaras. What he really means is that in every story of Baba in Sai Satcharitra, there are so many hidden pearls of knowledge that will help you raise your awareness and bring you to a state of wisdom.

When times are tough, Baba's words offer solace to his children. Baba's stories represent ways of living a simple life of honesty, integrity, and truth. It helps in expanding consciousness, and getting free of attachments that bring pain and suffering. Once you begin to read his book, you will notice subtle differences in your ways of thinking and every time you read it, you will find and understand new knowledge which will enrich your being and free you of your karma. You need to imbibe his teachings in your daily life and make it a part of your personality.

Sai Satcharitra is a sacred text he wrote through one of his child who is close to his heart –Shri Hemadpant. Sai aimed to make himself feel close to his children who read it. Every time you read the book, you will find new teachings and get your answers.

It's a transformative book that can help clear blockages in your life. Please read it in full awareness and be in the chapter entirely, and do not let your mind wander in different thoughts. You will also need to imbibe the knowledge in your daily life to find relief and be a true Sai Bhakta.

Sai Baba says, "Don't read my Sai Satcharitra blindly as a text just to complete it 11, or 21 times. Read it slowly, absorbing each and every word I have written in that text. The words themselves will heal you, free you of your suffering, and bring miracles into your life. Live the teachings of the text in your daily life. Every story has a hidden gem and you will get great insights to your own life through these stories. Breathe the stories and become a part of the time when I walked the Earth in the form of Sai Baba. You will get to know the truth. You will begin to release the illusion that keeps you bound in the samskaras. When you receive a chapter in a parayan to read, there is a message in it from you that will give you a clue to healing your life. My stories will liberate your soul to merge with the Light (Parvardigar). It will address your subtle denials, resistances, and deep unconscious mind. It will free you from bondages of previous birth, curses and vows you carry in your subconscious mind. My stories will make you feel loved, acknowledged, and supported and they will help you cross the oceans, reach the shores, and anchor your life in a great way. Make sure to absorb the knowledge and wisdom I share freely and drop the superficial and worldly life. Maya will try and entangle you in her clutches of samsara. My stories will open your vision to higher truths, Keep your life simple and authentic. Shed the extra frills and fancies as they will keep you distracted from your goal. Learn from your life and share your learning as pearls of wisdom with others, and you shall be free!!"

Your Beloved,
Sai Baba

Samskara - Negative Beliefs
Bhakta - Devotee Of
Parvardigar - The Lord
Maya - Illusion
Samsara - The Third Dimensional World

Om Sai Ram

Chapter 6

Dissolve Your Ego

What is Ego? The ego is a mask you wear over your deepest fears. Your overconfidence may actually be a mask for your low self-worth. Your overly talkative personality may be just a mask for your inner chaos and conflicts. Your demonic appearance (tyrant or harsh) may actually be a mask for your insecurities. How many masks do you wear? One day, will come when these masks will shatter and reveal your true nature. You are meant to face your fears and shed your egos.

Hold Sadguru Sai Baba's hand and learn to see the larger picture. You are here to get out of your comfort zone and take a plunge into the unknown to follow your passions. You are here to tap into your gifts (skills) and offer them to the world. You are born with a life purpose and to walk the path of truth. Sai Baba is here to shield your vulnerabilities and show you the mirror through Sai Leela, so you can make your weaknesses your strengths. Hold his hand, and he shall never fail you.

Many times, you might not be aware that you are wearing a mask, or you may be living in denial. At such times, Sai's blows are harsh, intending to remove the veils of the ego so your true self can emerge and become humble. The more you resist, the more painful the process. The more you understand that it's Sai Leela and keep asking yourself what you need to learn from the process, the easier the transformation from the egoistic mind to the higher mind. It opens the antechambers of your heart, and compassion flows through you.

Sai says, "Ego is like an onion, and many layers will have to be shed until you reach your soul's core. The transformation process is akin to a caterpillar becoming a beautiful butterfly. At such times of pain and suffering, your eyes should be only on me, as it's only me who shall take you across this ordeal. The more faith (Shraddha) and patience (Saburi) you develop, the easier it will be for you to evolve. Your true self is the pure essence of the Light of God (Parvardigar), and once you complete this awakening process, you shall look back and see what I meant. Your ego is only your personality, your soul is the Light. The more you work on your ego, the higher you will ascend. Many times, you will feel stuck, and people around you will project your roadblocks, but that too will be my test (Leela) to see if you pass my test. The subtlest ego will have to be shed by forgiveness. Forgiveness eliminates all the residues of karma of holding on to false samskaras and thus reveals the true nature of your soul. I will help you through the process of spurging. You are here for your rebirth (awakening) to an elevated consciousness. That must be your ultimate goal. I will make you fall to your knees and then to your ground to rise to the Light. I shall await your rise. I shall wait patiently for you to cross the bridge and come to me. I do believe and trust in you my child. I belong to you, my child, just as you belong to me. I am here to serve you. I will always stand by your side."

Your Beloved,
Sai Baba

Sewa - Service

Om Sai Ram

Chapter 7

Service To Sadguru Sai Baba

We don't choose to serve Sai; Sai chooses us to serve him. Only when Sai wants it you will be selected to serve him, and when that happens, accept that offer. It's the best thing that will ever happen in your life to be chosen by Sai to spread the Light. Refrain from knowing how you will manage so many troubles on your own. This is also one of his Leelas. He will choose you, make you his channel, and work through you.

You are not the doer! You must learn to be an empty flute, and Sai Baba will blow his Light through you. You, too, will be cleansed of your karma in the process as the Light will pass through you to reach all, and in return for your service, the blessings you will receive from 'The Children of Sai' will ease off your karma. It's a very humbling process, full of gratitude.

The biggest challenge is to keep the 'I' aside when you begin to serve Sai and replace it with 'Nothingness', for it's not you doing anything. The 'Doer' is Sai Baba. Once you understand this concept, you will remain humble.

Trust his choice when he chooses you. There is always a higher purpose in what he does. When in service of humankind, you will accumulate good karma, and you will slowly negate your bad karma. Life will begin to ease out for you. There will be immense wisdom that you will accumulate in the process.

Om Sai Ram

Sai says, "I ask my children for the service only of which they are capable of. I will never ask you to do something you cannot handle. No work is worse or better than the others. Each work is assigned to you as per your readiness and the skills you carry. Being in my service can help you redeem your karma quickly. Whatever situation you are in, how many challenges you face, and how much garbage people throw at you, you should focus on my service only; I will handle and clear the rest. I will create a new beginning for you, my child. This is your service to me. Do not compare what I have assigned to another. No one is better or worse than you. I do not judge or compare. You are special in your own way. This service to me will increase your quotient of grace and blessings from me, accelerating your life growth. I am with you wherever you go, even across the seven seas. I will send the right opportunity for you to serve me, you must pick it up without resistance. It can be in any form, like looking after the sick, feeding a poor family, becoming a channel for my messages, writing a book, maybe doing sewa in a temple, looking after an orphanage, or donating to a blind school. Whatever I ask, you must perform. In this way you will accumulate blessings to redeem any negative karma. It will make your positive karma more strong and you may be able to bear life lessons more better. Your debts will soon be cleared. I am waiting on the other side to merge with you."

Your Beloved,
Sai Baba

Chapter 8

Dhuni–The Eternal Flame

DHUNI is the sacred fire burning in Dwarkamai for the last 150 years. Baba created this Dhuni for a divine purpose. He made it and left it burning eternally for us to burn away all the negativity and sins. It's the holy flame that burns the bad karmas of Sai Baba's children to ashes, and the product of this Dhuni is Vibhuti. The Vibhuti is the most miraculous tool that Sai has left for us and has the most magical effect on Baba's children. It clears negative energy, shields it, and protects the one who applies it.

Sai left his legacy in this miraculous form to help us even after he is long gone from this third-dimensional Earth. There are many stories as to how the Vibhuti has created miracles and healed the sick, and protected all from evil and any harm. The Dhuni is the sacred flame, which is very powerful and can destroy anything negative while retaining the positive. Don't hesitate to use this holy flame to cleanse yourself from any vices, evil, or karmic residues. It's the magical flame which can help in many ways. It can clear the energy field of people holding emotional baggage and mental residues, which can create health issues in the long run.

You have to visualize the Dhuni and work with it. The Dhuni is also a reminder to destroy the ego and remain humble, as one day, we will all perish in flames and become ashes. We leave the material belongings, attachments, and desires on this Earth, as they never belonged to us anyways, and go back home only with the richness and lessons of our souls.

Sai says, "I have created the Dhuni and the Vibhuti for your benefit. Use and distribute the Vibhuti freely. They are also a gentle reminder that your ego is of no use; it's the 'I' that you carry with you which is the cause of all problems. Throw it into the Dhuni, and you shall emerge peaceful and happy. The Dhuni is a gift from me to you, and you must respect it and believe that it can help you eradicate all the negativity. Have faith in its power. I am present in it; I am just a call away. It's the eternal flame from the realms of Devas – the Agni. My Vibhuti will keep reminding you of the detachment with every desire you have. I have worked all my living years working on it, so I can make it available even after I am gone. The miracles of my Vibhuti will be heard from all corners of the world. It's available infinitely, as a source for you. My power lies in it. They are tools for healing and a very powerful source for resurrecting health. If you can't find it or don't have it with you for some reason, take my name and burn some incense sticks, then take the ashes, charge it with my name to become as powerful as the Vibhuti of my Dhuni. Chant my name in it, and all work can be accomplished."

Your Beloved,
Sai Baba.

Paramam Pavithram Baba Vibhuthim
Paramam Vichitram Leela Vibhuthim
Paramartha Ishtartha Moksha Pradhanam
Baba Vibhuthim Idam Asrayam

Vibhuti - Hoky Ashes
Dhuni - The Sacred Fire

Chapter 9

Test Of Time

Trials and tribulations come as a test. When you feel you are cornered and no one understands you. When name-calling occurs along with blame games and your near and dear ones have gone against you. Remember that this is a TEST. It is one of the toughest tests of ascension and union with Sadguru.

Tests assigned to you according to your karmic baggage. Sometimes, you are left alone to fend for yourself emotionally and even financially, as all your blood relatives may have passed away. Maybe some of you have seen tragic deaths in your family. If you can manage to stay afloat through these types of challenges, practice faith and patience, and see the larger picture through It all, you will pass the test with flying colors.

If you can manage to hold Sai's hand through it all, and even if it lasts for maybe a day, weeks, months, years, or even a lifetime, keep only Sai in your sight at all times, come what may, retaining the Shraddha (Faith) and Saburi (Patience) by doing Naam Jaap, going inwards to your heart's center and remaining connected to Sai's heart, you will achieve a massive clearance of your karma.

Focus only on unity with Sai, and nothing can touch you. In your limited mind, you may wonder why you are experiencing all this. You may have multiple questions but no answers. Make sure you do not allow the external voices to blow you down. If the storm comes, it will go away too. That's the ultimate truth of life.

These tests come in accordance with your karmic baggage. Do not allow trauma to set in. Use this time to build more faith and resilience.

Sai says, "When I incarnated on Earth and lived in Shirdi, these people did not leave me either. They kept pointing fingers at my authenticity. They blamed me for being a fraud and many other labels were attached to me. I had allowed them to do it because my heart and soul knew who I was. This blame didn't deter my faith in my Parvardigar (Lord). I kept focusing on the Light I had come from, and everything just passed by as a storm would pass by. I did the duties given to me by my Parvardigar with complete faith and undeterred focus. People also tested the eternal devotion of Meera, the esteemed devotee of Lord Krishna. She was given poison to drink to test her devotion to the Lord. She didn't flinch an eyelid. She didn't get affected either by the abuse or by the poison. Her faith was 'atal'. If you stay strong with me, then whatever stones are hurled at you, nothing will hurt you. You have my protection. These people are ignorant and do not know what they are doing because their level of awareness is low and their hearts are shut. They cannot see the truth. Do not feel like a victim due to these people's behavior. Make a castle out of the stones hurled at you. You stay calm and in your center; no harm shall come unto you. I shall carry you in my arms and across. Pray for such people and ask Parvardigar (God) to open their hearts, as they don't know what they do. You surrender to me; surrender to the Light! My Light is replenishing you right now!"

Your Beloved,
Sai Baba

Atal - Immovable

Chapter 10

When My Desire To Live Has Ceased

It is said that most of us will have a moment in their entire lives when our desire to live is overcome by the urge to give up and die. Life may present extreme situations that might make you feel like it's enough and that you do not want to live anymore. Your mind conceives different plans of action to die. Some of you may have even attempted it once or twice in your lowest moments. That's the power of Darkness; it will always want you to give up. The Light will always pick you up from your lowest point and uplift your spirits.

Now the question is, "What do you do when you feel like life has betrayed you?" You feel like you are a victim of life. How do you react when your repeated appeals and prayers to your Sai seem to fail? You may think that even Sai doesn't love you because if he did, he wouldn't leave you alone in such circumstances. You may feel as if Sai Baba has abandoned you. Your future seems bleak and hopeless. You cannot understand how you will pass through these challenging times. It seems no one around you understands you and your problems, and there appears to be no solution in your mind. You feel alone and unloved.

You may not even believe it if someone told you your Sai Baba might never leave you. He can see what your eyes cannot see, and the situation may have some higher truths that you may not understand in your lower mind. This is the time when Sai comes even closer to you. He speaks directly now. If you can hear Baba and hold on to him during this drowning phase, you will instantly be removed from the turmoil. He will carry you in his arms in times like this; hold on to him.

The Awakened Sai Within You

Sai says, "My Dear child, I know you are feeling abandoned, but believe me, I have not left your side for a moment. Even though you get angry at and curse me, I do not leave your side. Does a mother leave the side of the child who curses her? My love for you is very vast. Whenever you feel hopeless and think of giving up your life, NEVER GIVE IN TO THAT DARKNESS. I am forever holding your hand. Focus only on your Sai's Light. My Light will protect you like a shield in all your misfortunes. I have warded away much more than you can imagine. What you are going through is only thirty percent of what should have happened. I stand before you and absorb your problems before they reach you. Your Sai stands with you forever; do not worry. in your darkness, your connection with me is less. Think of me only. Read my stories, chant my name, hear my Artis, and I shall save you. You are wiping your karma when you are going through your challenges, and only the brave can handle such storms. Life and death are in the hands of your Sai. I am the writer of your script. Your challenge is to stay afloat; however difficult it may sound right now. I choose your death, and I choose how your life should be. You surrender your life to me. Think of a rose, and I shall be by your side instantly. The rose is a reminder of my love for you. Do not give up hope; the best is yet to come. When things get better you will understand how my words are like amruta to you in times of vish!"

Your Beloved,
Sai Baba.

Amruta - The Elixir
Vish - The Poison
Arti - Songs Of Love For The Lord Incorporated In The Puja

Chapter 11

When All Is Well In My World

In bad times, you tend to pray and remember God, running from one temple to another. But when you are having a good time, you forget Sai's name and get engrossed in the material world. When you have problems, you become sad, and you become delighted when everything is going well for you. This is called living in a world of duality. This way, you will keep attracting the opposite, while this dance of happiness and sadness will continue forever.

The key to growth is to balance all the time—allow the good times and bad times to pass by; both should be handled with grace and gratitude. Every moment should be appreciated— "Sai, thank you for everything you show me; the good times and the bad times. Sai, it's all in your grace". You can be peaceful if you can balance all the moments with gratitude. Gratitude to each breath, each experience, each relationship, the healthy body, the food you eat, the house you live in, every drop of water available to you, and all the money you spend, even if it's the last penny.

Allow gratitude every time you take a fresh breath of air and every time you release your breath. This won't happen in a day; it needs to be built up slowly each day, striving for more and more. It requires effort and a conscious awakening. And the more gratitude you possess, the more you will be happy and have abundant grace. Talk to him daily and keep yourself in his Sharan at all times. His grace will bestow on you more happiness and abundance.

Sai says, "I tell you not to cry or laugh more than is required. Try to maintain inner calm and inner strength. Maintaining a balance is the key to growth and prosperity. Have gratitude flowing at all times 24x7 from your unconscious mind to your conscious mind.. My dear child, gratitude is to be given at all times, good or bad. it must become your second nature. When you are in gratitude, grace will fall on you abundantly. The result is a balanced, centered space. Nothing should affect you beyond a certain degree. Free yourself of certain attachments, Dukha (sadness) and Sukha (happiness), and I will free you of your mortal body. You need to break down the ego to maintain this balance. Vanish the pride and ego, and you will be free from pain and suffering. Peace will follow you everywhere. Ananta Sukha (eternal joy) will fill your heart. Enlightenment will lead you to Moksha (liberation). My grace falls on those who are filled with gratitude. Gratitude opens the door to heaven. So, develop an attitude of gratitude, and you will be free. Time and tide are ever-changing, ever-evolving, and constantly shifting. The only constant is change. I hold your hand through all the change. I am your SAI – YOUR UNIVERSE. I will lead you across the worldly attachments towards God, towards the brilliant Light, and towards the enlightenment of your soul. Good times are times when you must feed the poor, develop compassion, and not get lost in the labyrinth of material desires."

Your Beloved,
Sai Baba

Dukha - Sadness

Sukha - Happiness

Ananta Sukha - Eternal Joy

Moksha - Liberation

Om Sai Ram

Chapter 12

My Never-Ending Problems

You have been praying for years and years, and you have done all that is required with complete faith to get relief from your situation. But come what may, you don't seem to have any relief, and you cannot see any Light in sight. You seem to face challenges day in and day out. One situation gets resolved, and another is waiting for you. You just can't relax.

You are holding on to Sai's feet firmly, but there is no respite. You seem surrounded by darkness with no ray of light in sight, and then you question your faith. You ask, "Sai, I am your child, and I pray to you with full dedication, but I don't see relief in my situation. How do you expect me to have patience? The messages you send me constantly don't seem to come true. Life is passing by, and challenges do not seem to end. Sai Baba, when will I be free from my problems?"

In the bleakness of this moment, you must understand that such challenging and tumultuous times are your soul's choices for clearing your karmic patterns. In fact, it's a blessing that in such harsh times, Sai Baba is by your side, holding your space, so you can go through this with ease. Review your life, observe how Baba stood by you, and remember how he showered sparks of light into your darkness. Do not blame Sai Baba. Instead, hold him more strongly so you can get through these times. Always remember that this too shall pass. It may be long, but not forever.

Your karma is keeping you in this turmoil, but Sai is holding you through it. Trust it!

Om Sai Ram

Sai says, "My child, your karmic baggage is vast, and you are a strong and brave soul. I stand by you like a rock, holding you through your pain and suffering. My wisdom and light will always guide you. Don't I send you messages in your dreams and talk to you? Haven't I sent you the right people to help you? Your soul is evolving quickly, and my assistance aids the process. Never think your Sai is not listening to you. Year after year, the same problems indicate you have to do things differently and break some patterns within you to bring about the change. There may be patterns that continue from generations or birth, and you may have chosen to resolve them. These patterns will be very visible and stubborn. They will create havoc in your life. They will keep rearing their head to stare at your face until you don't address them. You also need to open up your consciousness to receive my help. Many times, you reject it, thinking I will bring about the change magically. But I have sent support, and you must recognise it. Things that you have to change, you must realize. You have to work on them consciously. That what you resist always persists. My eyes follow you everywhere. I keep sending you support through messages to remind you that you are not alone. Sometimes you have to endure pain to develop virtues like patience and faith - Shraddha and Saburi. Be resilient on your journey. When gold goes through the process in the furnace, only then does it shine and obtain its high value. You, too, are shining your atman (soul) to a higher vibration and a better radiance. Keep up the excellent work. Your Sai is always with you."

Your Beloved,
Sai Baba

Atman - Soul

Chapter 13

When Your Wishes Are Not Granted

Often, it is seen that someone is finding it difficult to conceive, is not getting married, or is unable to own a house; they still keep praying to Sai but with no results.

Prayers may sometimes go unanswered or be answered after much effort and delay. Do you feel Sai Baba doesn't love you? Or does he love his other children more than you? It's like a child asking for chocolate; a mother refuses as she knows it's not good for the child's health. The child gets angry at the mother and feels as if the mother doesn't love him. The cognitive ability of the child is very low; he is not equipped to understand why the mother doesn't give him what he desires. He may perceive this as evidence that his mother doesn't love him. Sai Maa may not give you what you are asking for, even if you cry like a child. Your consciousness may not be equipped to understand the reason he is holding it back from you. Sai will not grant your wishes just because it's your desire, and ruins your life, or interferes with your karma. He can see the bigger picture. You will wonder, how does asking for a baby or wanting to get married harm me? Sometimes it's not your destiny to have it, and Sai may be saving you from some pain attached to it. Just because you have asked for it, there can be consequences with it. The baby might have an early death or a prolonged illness, or he may cause pain and suffering for the parents in many ways. Sai knows what's best for you.

When you ask for a wish to be granted, let go of the results and surrender that whatever happens will be for the highest good of all involved.

Sai says, "My child is in pain, I am in pain. I suffer as you suffer. I cry for my children when they get through their hardships. Believe in the perfect timing and never doubt the process. Just believe your Sai is with you, working to move things in your favor. But I cannot grant you certain things that are against your karma. They will only give you pain and suffering. Let go of your suffering and align your will with my will. I respond to all equally. You may feel I fulfill other people's prayers faster than yours, but I am only responding to your past karmas. I want you to work on your karma and energetic imprints, clear your cellular memories, and make space for my grace. Sometimes, if your wishes are not granted, have a positive attitude and know you are protected from something. So, the gratitude quotient must always increase with time. Believe me, my child, your Sai is only doing his best to make the impossible possible. I am always working things out for you. Nothing is hidden from my eyes. Trust my decisions, which will always be for your highest good. At the end of each prayer, say, "Sai, if it happens, it's good; if it doesn't happen, it's very good, as my Sai, you know the best!" Let go of the outcome and attachment fully. I will create miracles in your life!!"

Your Beloved,
Sai Baba

Chapter 14

Shed The Ignorance

The purpose of your soul's journey to Earth is to grow and evolve. But just as a soul takes a human birth, the veils cover you with ignorance, and the five senses distract you from your goals and create illusions. You lose yourself, creating separation and suffering. You fall prey to worldly desires. You run after them, trying to fulfill them, but still do not get peace. You fulfill one, then you run after another. It's a constant race within you to compete with others. You will notice, come what may, that you do not attain peace.

Your goal should be to merge with Sai. You should remember your soul's journey and Sai's importance in that. Being with Sai is the only thing that will guarantee you eternal peace. Your eventual desire should be to shed your ignorance, which leads to a path of pain and suffering, so you can clear your karma and free your soul from these bondages of worldly desires.

Your chants should be focused on attaining spiritual freedom. Enrich your soul with the wisdom of Sai Baba through his books, like Sai Satcharitra and many others, through chanting, etc. Imbibe the teachings of Sai in your daily life, in your every thought, and in your every breath. You will free your soul from the cycle of life and death.

Being a child of God, you must devote your time to evolving, spend time in his teachings, and try to change your life by being a karma yogi. Life is a school, and the seeker in you must always keep seeking and evolving. It will help you transcend.

Om Sai Ram

The Awakened Sai Within You

Sai says, *"Your life is a gift to you to assimilate and learn important soul lessons. Your Sai holds you through your turbulences so you can break your patterns and learn your lessons. Sometimes I must become your harsh mother who scolds you to study to pass the tests. If you look at your life experiences, you will see a pattern emerging that will lead you to your soul's core lesson that your soul has chosen to learn in this lifetime. Ignorance can bring you pain and suffering, and even I cannot help you much. You constantly ask me, "Sai, Why me? Sai, when will all be fine?" Ignorance will lead you to suffering, even if you cannot understand why. Enlightenment will come from the expansion of the mind and a change in perception. You need to constantly chant my name and read my stories to derive wisdom and free yourself from the clutches of karma and attachments. My one touch on your hand can raise your consciousness to immense heights. I can free you in the blink of an eye. But even I have to wait for the divine timing. Only when you are ready to break the patterns can I bring about a change in your life. I wait for you to stop praying for material gains and begin to pray for your soul's ascension. abundance will follow as a result of ascension. My Parvardigar never leaves you empty. Then you will begin to merge with me. Love all fellow beings. Never stop being good, and you will be free."*

Your Beloved,
Sai Baba

Chapter 15

Sai Is My Savior

"I"- This word denotes your ego mind. You believe, I do this, and I do that. You feel like you are going to a Sai temple or Shirdi. Little do you understand that you are not going; Sai Baba is calling you to his abode. If he doesn't want it, you cannot even lift a finger. You do not choose "Sai"; Sai chooses you as his child! And you are even more lucky if Sai Baba chooses you as his instrument to do his various jobs to serve humanity at large.

Sai chooses you to make a larger plan. It helps you to redeem your karma. He is allowing you to become an empty flute through which he can play his beautiful music. If you have an ego that says you are the chosen one, drop it now and remain humble. Your visit to the "Sacred Land of Shirdi" is actually him calling you. Without his calling, you cannot even enter Shirdi. By removing the "I" from the doership, you ascend your soul to a higher awakening.

By serving Sai, your higher heart opens, and you begin to learn unconditionally. Sai sees all equally without judgment and expects us to do the same. For him, all his children are one. When 'He' guides your life to serve others, it's a blessing in disguise. Sometimes you may realize this later; the best way to be is to trust that Sai is looking after you. Your personality has to drop, and your authentic self must emerge. That's what Sai wants from you.

When your soul is purified, then all you will emit is the light of Sai. The soul emerges to unite with the consciousness called Sai Baba, which we call "The Awakened Sai Within Us".

Sai says, "I have a relationship with you across many lifetimes. I walk with your soul across a million suns. I have been with your soul from the beginning of its journey, helping you learn. Didn't you recognise me the moment you saw me? Don't you know I am with you when I come in your dreams? I am always attracting your attention so you always focus on remembering me. Don't think that you are the doer. I am the doer of your life. I hold the strings of your life in my hands, including all the bad experiences and people who are not good to you. I create them for your karma clearance. Every time you come to Shirdi, I call you. Without my permission, you cannot enter or exit Shirdi. Whenever someone offers you a ride to Shirdi, it's my doing. Next time someone offers a ride to Shirdi, remember I am calling you. Each time you are distracted, keep bringing your focus back on me and me only. This way, you will receive more than you deserve. I reside in your heart. Once I reside in your heart, tie me to it with your faith and love and I will be a prisoner in your heart for life. I will do my duty of refilling your heart with the love of my Allah, and I will forever make your soul and heart shine like a million suns. I am your father and mother across many lifetimes, so have faith in me. Be my channel, and your life will rise to a level of bliss. Your life is in my hands, and I will lead you across!"

Your Beloved,
Sai Baba

Chapter 16

The Act Of True Surrender

The human mind is not trained to surrender. The lower your vibrations are, the more you need to control your life. The intensity of your need to control depends on the intensity of your fears and your inability to have faith in the flow of your life and life experiences. When the "I" is stronger, you neither believe in God nor trust life or the universe.

The ego is a mask for deep-seated fears, letting go of trauma, anger, expectations, unfulfilled desires, the need to see the results, and much more. Surrendering is an art that takes a long time to master. Your worrying doesn't end, and your inner chattering goes on. You keep feeling angry, depressed, and fearful. You cannot feel happy; you feel as if life is unfair. You constantly try to control the circumstances by clearing, praying, and healing. You keep clearing one level, and another appears. You feel a false sense of self-worth.

Every day, keep saying, "Baba, I surrender to you!" How about not doing and just being? How about just being an observer and allowing things to pass by and take their natural course of action? When you say, "God, why me?", you can change it to, "God, as you wish!" Instead of asking for desires to be fulfiled, can you ask God to give you the strength to face your challenges?

True surrender happens when you learn to let go and can genuinely accept wherever you are. Owe up your life and surrender to Sai Baba; he will take care of everything.

Sai says, "Child, do you think you are surrendering to me? But then you are constantly worrying about HOW things will change. This HOW is a reminder that you still need to submit deeper to me. My two gifts, Shraddha (Faith) and Saburi (Patience), will take you closer to surrender. Each step taken with Shraddha and Saburi will bring you closer to me each day. Watch me as I surrender to Allah. Have you noticed I only observe and do not judge you? You must aim to come to my level to merge with me. That's the only way up. Surrendering has many benefits: it teaches you detachment and clears your illusions too. You transcend your lower emotions like anxiety, fear, anger, depression, and self-loathing. Every moment will not be an easy task to do, but you must walk the path following my orders. Surrender your worries to me; you will be happier and more stable in all circumstances. Your personality will change, and a better life will flow at ease for you with my grace. True surrender offers many gifts for you!! Surrendering is a process that takes years to accomplish. It cannot be achieved in one day. The measure of your fear is the measure of your quotient of surrender. They are correlated with each other. Measure your fears often to understand your level of surrender. The day you achieve a calm and fearless state of mind and embrace your life as my Prasadam, you will have achieved true surrender."

Your Beloved,
Sai Baba.

SURRENDER TO THE HOLY FEET OF SAI BABA –
A TRUE SURRENDER

OM SAI RAM

Chapter 17

Sai Baba's Jholi

Sai always carries a Jholi with him. It holds within it numerous etheric gifts for us.

It's also for surrendering the problems to Sai. Sai Baba is like a magical being of light who can create what you desire and release all your worries and problems. Here is a small visualization technique to surrender your problems in Sai Baba's Jholi:

Sit down in a lotus position and be very comfortable. Take your time to calm your mind and bring yourself into balance. Begin by focusing on your breathing in and out and allowing the breath to take over the mind. Your cognitive mind is beginning to slow down with each and every breath. This way, you reach a no-mind state. See yourself in an open meadow and invite Sadguru Sai Baba into your space. Watch him walk over towards you. He has his Jholi with him on his shoulder. Thank Baba for coming to you when you called. Begin by talking about your problems with Baba. Say it with a lot of clarity. Speak to him as you would with a father or a friend. Now tell Baba that you wish to surrender your problems to him in his Jholi so he can take care of them from now on. Now see him open his Jholi and see your problems—the energy of the issues, wherever it's stored in your body—moving out into Baba's Jholi. Feel yourself becoming lighter and lighter as the problems leave you and move into the Jholi.

Thank Sai Baba, and see him open his palms to bless you. See a ray of golden light leave his palm and enter your heart to fill up your entire body with golden light. Allow this process to be complete and for Sai's grace and light to fill you. Thank Baba for this wonderful opportunity, and slowly open your eyes.

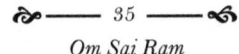

Om Sai Ram

The Awakened Sai Within You

Sai says, "There is a reason I carry this Jholi with me. It takes away all your problems and worries. Remember to give me your problems whenever you are under extreme stress or having sleepless nights; I travel with you wherever you go. I stand by you, day and night. I make things happen for you. I am listening to your worries, endlessly. My light will guide you always. My Jholi also has so many etheric gifts for you. You will receive it in divine timing. I have many different Astras to present to you, that will help you with your problems. My Jholi also holds many non-tangible gifts like strength, resilience, patience, faith, happiness, abundance, and much more. Ask, and you will receive. Never hesitate to ask me what you want. Open your palms to receive, and I will forever pour my grace on you. I am your father, don't you ever forget that. As soon as you surrender your worries to my Jholi, consider that you are liberated from that problem. You will see they vanish for good, from your life. Once your samarpan is complete, I will offer you the gifts. Once you receive them, place them in your heart forever and use them in times when life feels like a storm. You shall see relief. In tough times, you remember me, so in good times, also chant with me. My Jholi is your magical bag. Trust and believe, and you will feel blessed."

Your Beloved,
Sai Baba

Jholi - The Sack Sai Baba Carried On His Shoulder
Astras - Tools
Samarpan - Surrender

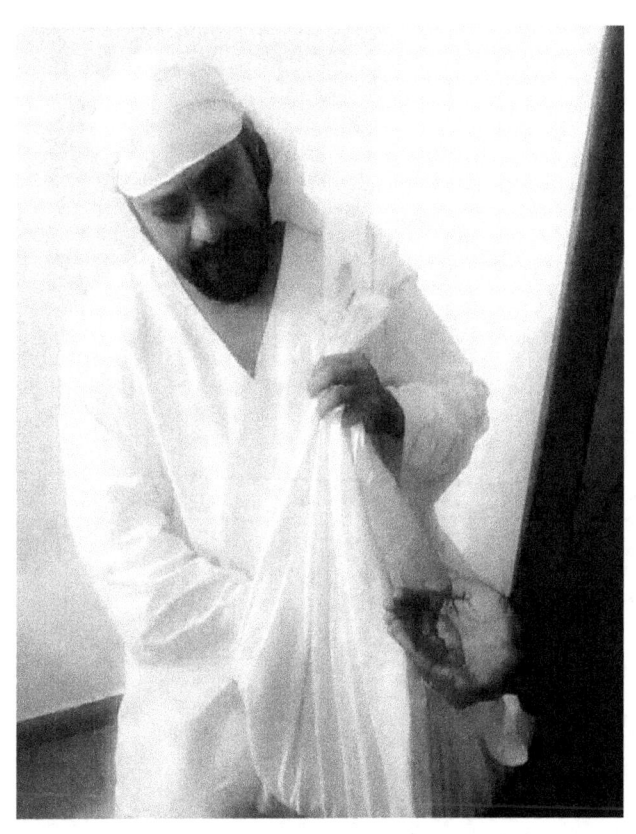

SAI BABA WITH HIS JHOLI

OM SAI RAM

Chapter 18

When Sai Baba Tests Your Patience

A challenging situation that doesn't seem to end!!! A wish that is just not being granted by Baba!! Maybe your challenge is just not clear. Your harsh environment is breaking you down every single day. Your situation may not be ending; your challenges are just as bad. You wonder why Baba is not hearing your prayers. Why is Sai not granting you any resolutions year after year? Baba will indeed bless you with relief in divine timing.

Just as a baby needs nine months in a mother's womb to be developed enough to be delivered into the world, the same way, it takes a certain amount of time to travel from one destination to another. Similarly, Sai always watches over you and understands your situation. Even he must wait for the right time to deliver your wishes. He is your Divine Father, and he only means good. These challenging experiences are here to teach you specific lessons. You must understand that these difficult people and situations mirror your inner psyche. There are certain things you owe up to and need to take charge of your life with Sai Baba holding your back.

Sai Baba helps those who help themselves. Accept the responsibility of your life and see how life changes for you. You can be a co-creator with Sai; wait patiently, allow the experiences to unfold, and see how life transforms for you. There is a thin line between manifesting and being a co-creator with Baba. The latter will happen only when you can align your will with Baba's will. Then life will flow for your highest good.

Sai says, *"My Child, your situation is a great learning center. Sometimes your disease is your karmic release. How can I take it away? It's doing good to you in the larger context of life's blueprint. You are releasing pieces of the baggage of many lifetimes through your suffering. I am holding you through it all. In the right time and space, your dreams will manifest into your reality. Always be good, even if negative people surround you. Never stop trusting, even if people are constantly breaking your trust. Do not fall to the level of your perpetrators. Do not be bad because people around you are bad. Maintain your dignity and your high level of thinking. Always remember that you are a child of Sai. You must maintain your name and dignity according to my standards. Have you ever seen me feel like a victim? You are also not a victim of circumstances; it's only divine play happening, or Sai Leela. Trust your Sai, no matter what. It's important to stay in your highest vibrations, whatever the situation. Maintain your calm and be centered on remaining in your power. Take charge of how you react and respond in a situation. My children who are connected to me have two core lessons - Shraddha and Saburi. It's the core of every life lesson and will take you back there. Patience is the key to all your problems.. Refrain from getting into old patterns of stress. Remember, everything will be alright, by grace, in the times to come!"*

Your Beloved,
Sai Baba

Chapter 19

What Should I Pray For?

You are praying and praying, and it still needs to be answered. The words you are choosing to pray for may need to be corrected. Many times, the focus needs to be in a better place. It's essential to pray with the right words, and there's also one important thing to note: "Never pray from lack; the energy that is going out emits the lack. Pray knowing you are in sync with the universe and as abundant as the universe."

For example, you must urgently reach for an appointment when it begins to rain heavily. You begin to pray, "Baba, stop the rain so I can reach the appointed destination." This is an incorrect way to pray. The correct way would be to ask Baba to help you reach the destination dry, safe, and in time for your appointment. Then surrender to Baba and see what he does to ensure you arrive safely. He may stop the rain, provide you with an umbrella, or send a car to get you across, etc.: this must be left to him to decide. We just have to state the end goal. The journey can be led by Sai.

Another important thing is that when you pray and ask for something, your actions and vibrations should be in sync with your prayers. Making the right move at the right time is very important. Say, for example, that you didn't take that lift that was sent for you. Did you pick up the signs and help given to you directly or indirectly? Sai can show you the way, but you must walk the path. Sai can help you clear pathways in your subconscious mind before your prayers. But there are specific patterns that you need to clear from yourself before you are answered.

Sai says, "I cannot intervene in your life unless asked. Your life is to be lived in accordance with your free will and destiny— blueprint. You ask, and I shall give it. So many times, I am waiting to deliver, but you either forget to ask me or are not focused on what you are requesting. Many times, you need clarification. Sometimes you ask for one thing and then you change your stance. You contradict your own prayers. Your prayers need to be consistent. I cannot give it to you immediately at times, so I patiently wait till you learn your lessons, are ready to receive them. I send many messages to you: through people, billboards, writings on taxis, and songs. You may see my photo or idol, and you will know you are at the right place and I am leading you. I keep sending you my assurances in different ways or forms. You think I do not answer or hear your prayers, but that's not true. You must understand what you are praying for and take full responsibility for the outcome and karma payback. Always pray for the highest good of all involved. You are not alone. You have a whole network of people connected to you in the form of family, friends, and your soul family. It's like a ripple effect. Your actions will also affect others. You are a piece of thread in a mesh of fabric that makes up the whole cloth. Your karma is taken by following your steps, walking the labyrinth called Life and your prayer can only be granted. I will always answer your prayers; I promise you that."

Your Beloved,
Sai Baba.

Chapter 20

Why Do Good People Suffer?

How often have we heard that good people suffer while the so-called bad people seem to be enjoying their lives? Many of you have this question: Have you always been good? Still, somehow you attract perpetrators into your life, and they don't even seem to get punished. In contrast, you feel your life only punishes you through these people.

First, the Master, your Sai Baba, doesn't have the concept of good or bad. Each one of you who prays to him is his Beloved child. Each one is playing their role in the larger scheme of things. The good people (according to your understanding of good or bad people) are now ready to complete their karmic cycle and are in payback mode. They are under Sai's wings and redeeming their karma at a breakneck pace. Their lives seem to be in turmoil and very dificult. If you look at them closely, they surrender to Sai and can see the larger picture.

Their test is to see Sai's Leela in everything around them. They are in the process of learning and karmic release. Their primary and most brutal lessons are patience, tolerance, and humility. Whatever you endure is your karma; no two souls' life paths can be compared.

Each one comes with a different plan. When the so-called bad people seem to enjoy their lives, they could be redeeming their past good karma, and their present wrong actions may be recorded for future redemption.

Om Sai Ram

Sai says, "In my eyes, they are all the same. I cannot judge you, as each of you has your learning and growth in your life path. All are mere experiences. You all, too, do not judge each other. Each one is playing their part in the larger picture. The mean perpetrator is also a soul in pain and a part of your divine plan. His heart is so shut that he cannot see the positive in anything. He seems to be enjoying his life, but he is in the world of Maya (illusions). The day these illusions break, he will repent and redeem you just as you are. He is an unaware soul, not awakened yet. You are a beacon of light, so when you come under my wings, you may feel that many issues have surfaced, and your purging speeds up. This might seem like a tough life. But you have come a long way and are in the so-called "Good" category. Your test is to be good, come what may. You need to hold your vibrations high, no matter what. You may feel you are suffering while others are enjoying themselves. You have a soul contract to release all this. It would be best to face the harsh environments, infirmed people, circumstances, judgment, blame games, and politics head-on. I am with you, holding your space while you redeem your karma and learn. Don't ever think that I will abandon you. Sai will help you pass your tests. I am teaching you faith and patience. These tests will make you stronger over time. Looking back, you will realize how far you have come. Learn faith (Shraddha) and patience (Saburi) and see how quickly you pass these tests."

Your Beloved,
Sai Baba.

Chapter 21

Tyrant Family Members

The most challenging lessons are learned in relationships with difficult family members; most of the time, they are the closest family members: a parent, a child, a spouse, or a parent-in-law. These relationships are ones one cannot run away from. Most of the time, there are no exits. They are someone you may need to put up with for most of your life due to unavoidable circumstances. They are adamant, and you may feel powerless and helpless when it comes to them. They are usually tyrants, probably living with patriarchal belief systems, having negative samskaras and usually enjoy seeing you in this weak state. They feel powerful when they see you helpless.

You are constantly hearing criticism from them. You feel traumatized by the constant harsh words being hurled at you. You sometimes cry in silence, wanting to maintain peace but you may be breaking down. You wonder what karma you did, to have to face so much harshness around you. You call Sai Baba to free you every day from this prison-like environment.

Your faith in Baba gives you the patience to wait in the hope that one day they will change, know your worth, and mend their ways. But that day doesn't come. You read Sai Satcharitra daily and visit the temples frequently, keep fasts, do rituals but the situation remains the same. You are exhausted and feel that maybe Baba doesn't love you.

Do you know what lessons you have to learn? Are you sure this life and these people are not your creation per the blueprint? Is Sai to blame for these people in your life?

Sai says, "My child, sometimes you come with a difficult life to redeem your karma, pay off all your debts, or break down your subtle ego. Yes, you carry a subtle ego in your auric fields—that last bit that needs to be released. All the ego and harsh words around you are a projection of your inner world. It's your choice whether you want to clear it. Just as a sculptor chisels and hammers a stone to make a beautiful statue, your life experiences make you a beautiful, shining soul by breaking you down completely, so you can renew your soul structure to a higher ascended vibration. Use this harsh environment to grow. Be like a lotus blooming fully and brightly in murky waters, it's a perfect example of how one can ascend beautifully despite all the ambiguity around them. Staying in your center and taking my name will give you relief. Let the pain become the bridge to enlightenment. Use this suffering as a tool for your ascension. How you react or respond is in your hands and none others. Do your best to show forgiveness to the people around you. Do not hold on to hatred. I am with you always. And when your pain and suffering grow, put them in my Jholi. I will take care of it, holding you through it all. Every act of karma has a shelf life. Just as good times end, bad times also don't last forever. Forgiving difficult people, and seeing them as victims of life, and sending light to them is your Dharma."

Your Beloved,
Sai Baba.

Dharma - Code Of Conduct

Om Sai Ram

Chapter 22

What Happens When We Curse?

It's so easy to curse someone; It's just like yelling a few words, and then it's over. You feel calm and relieved. Your ego has been satisfied that you have had the last say. But the consequences of your actions can last for many lifetimes. Yes! You heard it right. They will stay until you resolve and forgive. There is no relief from the person or the experience unless you forgive them. They can go on for lifetimes unless resolved.

Every action results from a thought. Every thought is constantly creating karma. The intention behind a curse can never be positive. Cursing someone when angry or jealous creates major entanglements for you with the person you have condemned. The consequences for the same have to be taken into account; if not in this lifetime, then in another one, but there is no escape.

Forgiveness has to be done; you have to open your higher heart to exude compassion, accept each human as they are, and free yourself from the cycle of this karmic knot. It's like a knot in your etheric cords and chakras. They can be generational curses that are coming down from generations. You must be born as blood relatives or create a relationship through marriage to continue the karma.

So it would be best to be careful and responsible for your words. Once they come out of you, words can never be taken back. They are like arrows shot from the bow; they can only make a wound. Speak words that spread love and light. Your language should heal everyone you speak to. Your magic should spread like the vacchan of Baba. Be the light that transmits Baba's light through you.

Sai says, "My child, you must control your tongue and anger. If you resort to these low-vibration defense mechanisms, your Sai cannot help you. I understand that, at times, they cause you so much pain, and your hurt is so huge, that you unintentionally bring a curse to your tongue. It only means you haven't yet fully surrendered to me. it also means that there are unhealed parts of you that are projecting in your victimiser. There is a need to clear your inner wounds rather than cursing someone. If your faith in me is strong, you will refrain from these curses, as they become spells and bind you. you will too be entangled in the same curse. Why are you entangling yourself unnecessarily? You need to bring my name to your lips. Let me take care of them. Let me free you from this. Leave it on me. Next time you are hurt and your heart is bleeding, place my name on your lips instead of cursing. Surrender this hurt in my Jholi and drop the need to take revenge, even with words. The tongue is the seat of Maa Saraswati. Do not misuse this power, even if you feel you have been wronged. Make sure your core stability is not shaken up, no matter how hard the troubles hit you. When you remember me, my aura will form a shield around you and protect you from all harm. Similarly, when someone curses you, say Sai Baba; you know better. Baba forgives him; he doesn't know what he is doing. Leave everything else on me. I shall deal with the rest. That's my job in your life if you have made me your master. Have faith. Sab ka bhala ho!!"

Your Beloved,
Sai Baba

Vachan - Promise

Chapter 23

When You Take Others Karma On Yourself

Your child, spouse or parent may suffer health challenges, and you cannot see them suffering. It's unbearable for you. You can feel their pain and feel overwhelmed by their situation. You then ask God to give you their share of problems and free them from that karma. You think you are acting out of love and creating good karma. But this is working in contradiction to the Law of the Universe.

Love does not say to take the results of karma of your loved one on yourself. They have come with that experience to learn and grow. They have a lesson there. You cannot stop them from learning their lessons, by taking their karma on yourself. You must allow them to learn from the process of their experience. You can pray to Sai to ease them out or support them while they go through it. You can hold their space. But do not interfere with their blueprint.

It's vital to remember that even though you are with the ones you love, you are separate in the body. Your life lessons are different. Imagine always carrying a child in your arms; that way, you will never allow them to learn to walk. Would that be correct on your part to interfere in their karmic path?

Your path should be to empower them to walk their path courageously. That will be your love for them. You must hold their space while they go through their karmic releases, not absorb and suffer for them.

Om Sai Ram

The Awakened Sai Within You

Sai says, "Your loved one may not believe in me, but they will always be a part of my family, just like you. Even if they do not pray to me, they are my responsibility as they are connected to you. You do not have to worry about them. I will hold them, heal them, and reduce their pain and karma. That job is mine; your job is just to pray to me. Have 'Sai Sai Sai' on your lips. Write a letter to me stating your concerns for the loved one. Look after them unconditionally. Please do not take their karma on your head. It will entangle your blueprint. You may have a blueprint that is different from what you are absorbing. These energies may clash and embezzle your life. You are not alone; you are connected to many people by Runanabhandha (connected by blood and heart) Every action of yours creates a ripple effect on everyone around you. That's why I never encourage you to carry others' loads on your head. Walking the path of higher consciousness and awakening the Sai within you is very important. Being my child, you do not need to fear for your loved one. Fear has served no one. Your act out of worry will create a negative effect. your act out of prayers and chanting will create a positive ripple in their life. Follow my ascension signals and allow these heavy energies to leave you now. Allow yourself to lighten up. Know your boundaries, even with your children, parents, or spouse. Know that you are one and yet separate. Loving oneself is as sacred as loving others. Neglecting oneself is equivalent to neglecting me, as I reside in you. Pray to me for your loved ones' problems. I will handle it. All you can do is pray!!"

Your Beloved,
Sai Baba.

Runanabhandha - Connected By Blood And Heart

Chapter 24

There Are No Shortcuts In Life

Life is a balance between a series of choices you make and the cosmic laws you need to follow. It's a balance between your destiny and your free-will choices. It's a fine line from your throat chakra to your third eye chakra. Your young blood may have many dreams and desires, which are not wrong, but maybe a bit too outstretched. You may even want to achieve it all in a short period of time. You believe you can disillusion reality and that you are the creator. So you can manifest what you want with the snap of a finger.

In reality, your desires are your illusion, and not otherwise. Your soul designs them to create learning. See things from a higher perspective, and you will notice that you face obstacles and challenges when you follow your dreams. When you begin to clear them, you will have great learning opportunities, you will encounter people who will help you, and there will also be a few people who may betray you. But each one will teach you something. If you want shortcuts, the journey's growth and protection are lost. These shortcuts can be very damaging in the long run.

Isn't it said that it's not about reaching your destination? It's about the entire journey that leads you to your destination; that's important as that guides you through your soul, your hunger, and your quest, which are directly correlated to your growth. Once you understand this concept, you will become mindful of your actions. Mastering your art and skills is important to gaining success. Success gained quickly will not last longer because it's not associated with experience and wisdom. It's important to keep learning while growing.

Sai says, "Taking shortcuts harms your soul's journey and growth. It's said to enjoy your journey (process) and not focus on your destination. The method of life is your school of learning. It spurges huge karmic baggage; you learn a few core lessons in your life. Keeping the task at hand and allowing the process to flow is important to redeem your karma. It's vital to have Saburi (patience). You can enjoy your process, learn your part, and yet complete your journey with grace and blessings. You can see it as a game, a challenge you need to cross and see it from an objective view. Choosing shortcuts may be dangerous and may not come from truth, integrity, and honesty. Nothing comes for free. You cannot resort to escapism, you will have to eventually face it, even if it means, you have to take birth again to redeem it. Everything you do has a consequence, every desire will create an accumulation of karma. Reasonable and good action will yield good karma, and wrong actions will create bad karma. Only I have the power to create shortcuts for you, if I will. Praying to me can ease out your long roads, blocks, and challenges. Only with my guidance and permission can you take shortcuts. Sometimes your long routes can be fruitful, and your little mind cannot see the larger picture. If you follow my guidance, my blessings will pour immense abundance on you, and you will achieve great heights and success. You will successfully pass all tests of time, take all the resources you require from me to keep you courageous and motivated. I am your beginning and the end!!"

Your Beloved,
Sai Baba.

Chapter 25

The Samadhi Grants Boon

Baba abandoned his physical form, leaving devotees in mourning on October 15, 1918, on Vijaya Dashmi. He was a Fakir revered all over the world, with an ocean of devotees scattered all over the world. At 2:30 pm that afternoon, Sai told Bayyaji that he was leaving this world and that his body must be buried in the Booty Wada, assuring him that he would protect his devotees from the other side. He was leaving his meager physical body, but his presence will be strongly felt when his devotees come for darshan. He will bless them and grant them boons. He breathed his last, giving charity and jnana to his children. He attained Samadhi.

The divine light that came out of Baba merged with Gurusthan, Dwarkamai, and Chavadi, who were already in the form of divine light. One part went to Gurusthan; the other went to Chavadi and settled there. The third went to Dwarkamai, and the fourth went to Booty Wada. These four powers represent the four Vedas and signify Sai's powers, which can command and heal the world. The physical body of Baba was buried in Booty Wada, and this became the Samadhi Mandir.

Baba gave instructions even after he left the body to his devotees on how he should be placed and what rituals must happen. He also instructed on how the Arti's should be performed. Baba resides in this Samadhi, a compelling place where one can immensely feel his presence. He grants wishes and helps his children sitting in this powerful, magnificent Samadhi mandir. He assured his devotees of his presence even after he would be gone.

Sai says, "I left my mortal body. Do not think I am gone. I exist. I exist in your every breath. I exist in every cell of you. I will always exist beyond this mortal body to be here with you all. You will feel my presence from time to time. You will feel me guiding you. I am the light that will keep you on your right path. Keep praying to me. Keep following my light, and you will never fail. Troubles will come. Challenges will be a part of your life. They are your karma, and you will have to redeem them. But my guidance follows you everywhere. If you travel to any corner of the world, you will feel my presence. I am spread among each and every one of my devotees. You will see the light in their eyes when they say, "Om Sai Ram". It's my code to recognize each other. Your fellow beings, Sai family will hold your hand and lead you to your destination. I will keep sending my people. You will notice they are my children, and you can rest assured you are on the right path and in the right hands. My divine blessings follow you everywhere. My Samadhi will fulfill your wishes. When you visit Shirdi, you will never go empty-handed. Make a wish in my Samadhi and surrender fully. Your Sai will always provide you with what you require. Do not forget to keep Dakshina as an exchange. Your Dakshina is a loan you need to repay me. It will help many people around the world. This Dakshina is a mere exchange of money that will bring abundance to you and clear your money karma. I grant you boons in my Samadhi. You are my child. Ask, and you will receive! "

Your Beloved,
Sai Baba.

Samadhi - Sai Baba Was Cremated Here
Gurusthan - Babas Samadhi Is Here
Dakshina- Offerings In Money

SAMADHI MANDIR – SHIRDI

OM SAI RAM

Chapter 26

The Gurusthan Initiates Into My Kingdom

The meaning of the word Gurusthan is the place where the Guru resides. This is the place where the tomb of Sai Baba is located. He would sit below a Neem tree and spend most of his time there. Neem is a very medicinal plant, and it's very healing to sit under it. Magically, the Neem tree leaves in the Gurusthan are sweet and not bitter. Baba sat there very often and meditated with his Guru's energies.

Once, some people dug up this area and found four burning lamps there. Baba told them it belonged to his Guru and asked them to shut the place again. No one knows who Sai's Guru was. Baba always respected this place. Anyone who lights incense sticks here and prays, their wishes would be fulfiled. The sacred fire was brought from Dwarakamai to Gurusthan daily, and the Sansthan Poojari lit the Dhuni.

Baba held this Neem tree to be sacred. This blessed tree was always ready, waiting for Baba to sit under her shade. It is believed that the Neem tree is the abode of the Goddesses, and it is also referred to as "Neenari". In 'Sai Mahima Sthothra', Upasani refers to this Neem tree as surpassing the 'Kalpa Vriksha' and showering Ambrosia with Baba's grace.

Baba constantly sat under this Neem tree when he first came to Shirdi. The leaves are oozing nectar because of their healing properties. Hence, devotees worship this tree and eat its leaves mixed with pepper and sugar, as it has curative properties. Many devotees are relieved of their ailments by eating the leaves of this tree. 108 Pradakshina of Gurusthan is done by many devotees early in the morning and at other times to destroy their bad karma, attain spiritual enlightenment, and fulfill their wishes.

The Awakened Sai Within You

Sai says, "I have left behind spaces that will heal you and your generations to come. If you visit Shirdi, you must go to Gurusthan and bow down to the tree. The crown chakra activation and initiation process happens, when your crown bows down to the tree, or my Padukas. It activates your ascension process and makes you ready for evolution. Breathing in the air in the space there will lighten your entire energetic system and clear your pathways for a better flow of energy absorption. Always make sure you sit in the open space and take my name. The Dhuni maa burning there also creates the right aura for cleansing your Prana. Applying the ash from that Dhuni will cleanse and always protect you. I am forever present in Shirdi. You might have my live darshan if you seek me. Or I may come in any form to test your faith if you recognise me. I will see how you treat me. The initiation process of the Gurusthan is my and your guru-disciple relationship cord. After this, you can chant my name which will bring you out of any hardships. Shirdi is a beacon of light. All my children will be called to Shirdi for a reason. They need to be in my Sharan. If they need to take my blessings, they will get called there by me. It's a process of karma clearance and grace deliverance. Only the blessed ones, whom I call, can only reach my place. I am omnipresent. Visit the Gurusthan and experience the bliss of my Guru darshan. I shall speak to you there. Speak of your woes to me and watch me give you answers to your problems."

Your Beloved,
Sai Baba.

Pradikshana - Circumbulating
Padukas - Slippers Sai Baba Wore
Prana - Energy

Om Sai Ram

GURUSTHAN – SHIRDI

OM SAI RAM

Chapter 27

Man Proposes, God Disposes

"Wahi Hota Hai Jo Manjoore Khuda Hota Hai!!" Everything eventually happens with the "Will of God". We have read or heard this, and we have often experienced this happening to us. It's a fact that we have to understand that, however much we may want something, we may not get it if it's not in alignment with our vibrations. And however much we don't want to be in a situation or a place, our karmas may not allow us to have relief. Then what must be the course of action? Don't think or act? Wait for God to show you the way. No! It means we must align our will with the divine will and know that despite all that happens to us, we must keep seeing the larger picture.

It would be best to keep moving, acting, and taking decisions while aligning your intuition with your logic. You need to know that life is supporting you, come what may. If things don't happen according to your desires, there will be a higher truth that you can't see at the moment. So many times, when you look back a few years, you realize why things didn't happen as they should have. You can see now how it would not have been for your highest good. But at that time, you were so heartbroken and lost that you questioned why God was doing this to you?

It's all part of the game called Life. Even when karma doesn't relieve you, you know learning is pending and you must complete it. It's challenging, but not impossible. Accept what comes your way with grace. Swim with the tide, not against it. Keep seeking, keep asking, keep praying, and keep healing. You might not know how that helps you at that moment, but one day you will see.

Sai says, "I am your well-wisher, not your tyrant. I do not punish you ever. Your blueprint and your past karmas keep you anchored in difficult situations. I help you through your process by holding your hand in the storm. The Parvardigar is indeed the one who writes your destiny, and you need to learn to be with the flow. Whatever you are destined for, it will happen. But your prayers and staying in my Sharan will help you go through it easily. The will of God is the highest. When you learn to let go of trying to control your life and stay with the grace of God, you will see miracles happen in your life. Then, even when you have the most deadly disease, you will recover and see profound healing. Miracles happen when you stay close to me. I will speak to Allah! I will speak to Parvardigar for you. I am the child of God, and if you are with me, you, too, are blessed. Walk the path of light with me. Eventually, "wahi hota hai" what God thinks is best for you. Stay calm and trust the process. It's said that no matter how much you think and plan, what is God's will is what eventually happens, and it's the duty of us meager souls to bow down to his wish and follow the path he has chosen for us. All conflict ends once you allow God to decide the path for you. How can that ever be wrong? It will give you peace and fulfillment. All the external mirrors collapse once you understand that you are a puppet in the hands of the Lord. I, your Sai, am with you forever, guiding you with the light."

Your Beloved,
Sai Baba.

Chapter 28

The Act of Offering Food to Sai Baba

When everything belongs to Sai, why do we need to offer food to Sai? When Sai is omnipresent and supreme consciousness, he might not want the food. Then what's the purpose of offering food to him? What do we have to learn from it? It's a way to train your subconscious mind to remember that you are not the doer. You are the puppet in the hands of Baba. It's a gentle reminder that you don't own the food or have done anything to get it on the table. It's only Sai's wish that you have received the food on the table. It's a way to show him and the universe our gratitude. This will always keep the ego in check, and one will always remain humble.

Offering food also opens the higher heart chakra to unconditional love. Baba says if you provide to all those who come to your door, including animals and birds, you have served him. This is also a reminder that everything is Brahman. We are all one consciousness. This will help you remain humble, grateful, and full of love for all fellow beings on Earth. The offering also reminds us that when we feed others, we get fed, as it returns to us in manifolds.

The oneness is amplified, and the heart chakra connects to Baba's heart, creating a higher, expanded consciousness of love and harmony within you. Even if you can join your hands and pray to him in gratitude before you eat your meal, you will always have his grace on you. Being a good human is very important. These acts teach good behavior in you, and the abundance will only grow. A small act of offering food to Baba can help us so much along the course of our soul's journey and also help our soul transcend after death. He will help you sail across the oceans so your soul can reach its destination. Baba never forgets someone who offered him his food before he eats himself.

Om Sai Ram

The Awakened Sai Within You

Sai says, "*Jo mujhe apni roti khilayega uski Jholi kabhi khali nahi jaayegi*". Whoever offers me his meals will always be abundant, as he would have attained the essence of Brahman. He would have allowed his consciousness to rise to me. I am consciousness itself. Being one with the living beings of the Earth will help you become one with me. Offering food to others is an act of unconditional love and will remind you that nothing belongs to you. You have come with nothing, and you will go back with nothing. What you will take with you are your acts of kindness and your evolved consciousness. This is a direct way to help your soul grow. You do me no favor by offering food to me. Only you can help yourself. Remain humble at all times. Remember, you are not the Creator. The higher source is the creator, the Parvardigar. So, remember to bow down to him and keep saying, '*Tera Tujko Arpan Kya Laage Mera.*' All that I received from you I offer it back to you, as I own nothing. I have come empty handed and shall go back empty handed. This will keep you grounded and egoless. My child offering food is the greatest way to evolve. The meal doesn't have to be elaborate. It can be simple. Your left hand shouldn't know what your right hand has donated. You don't need to announce it to the world. You do not need to be pompous about it. I have served as an actual example of my state of living. I have taken Bhiksha (alms) from five houses, cooked meals, and served everyone who came, including animals. This is to be adapted as a way of living. You will feel one with Parvardigar and me if you do this. *Sabka Malik Ek.*"

Your Beloved,
Sai Baba.

BAIJAA MAA OFFERING FOOD TO SAI BABA

OM SAI RAM

Chapter 29

The Sharanagati (Surrender) To Sai Baba

It's effortless to say I have surrendered, but building the quality of Sharanagati is a process; it needs to be built up and made a part of your character. Once your surrender is complete, there is nothing left to do. Being a good Bhakta to Sai requires Sharanagati. How does one attain Sharanagati?

To be a true bhakta, one must acquire all the qualities necessary to be a child of Sai. One also has to dispel all qualities that don't go in sync with being a true child of Sai. He will drop everything that's not ethical and true. Another step is to develop immense faith in Sai. The belief in him must be so impeccable that, come what may, it won't be shaken up in any circumstance. He knows Sai will protect and care for him even in the worst cases. He will not sit and worry about himself and his family. Instead, he will focus on chanting Sai's name and reading Sai Satcharitra.

A true child of Baba will serve others and follow the path of sewa assigned by Sai. He will not waste time worrying about himself and his family, as he will know he has God to take care of his needs. He knows that whatever action he performs, Sai is watching him and will reward him. He surrenders the end results–the fruits of his efforts–to Sai's hands. He will develop deep humility as he knows the actual doer through him is Sai Baba himself, as he knows we are limited. Being bound by time and space and it's important to have humility. Humility means unselfishness, and it's a true character of self-surrender. A true bhakta will strive to attain these qualities and follow the path of Sai Baba.

The Awakened Sai Within You

Sai says, "I am forever watching you. I watch your actions and your thoughts. I ensure you don't stray and are always on the right path. I keep bringing you on track. I allot you service for humankind so you can redeem your karma quickly and attain moksha to come home to me, forever in time. I will give you tests periodically, to check how much you have surrendered. I allot activities to develop your faith and resilience. My Leelas are known to you all. I assign you activities to see how you build confidence, humility, and resilience, and today, I will share a secret with you all, that is I never leave you alone in your tests. I will help you along the way. Don't think of me as a harsh father. I may seem tough but it's required to help you ascend. I am your nurturing mother. I am all you will ever need. When your relationships give you trouble, turn to me. I am your best friend. Talk to me. I will talk to you from my Samadhi. Look into my eyes, and you will see I am alive in every statue and photo you come across. I remind you of me constantly, in many ways. I am the Writer of your life. I have written your past, present, and future. No one can change it. Everything will happen as per my wish. When you learn to see the good in all circumstances, stop cursing me or life, and focus on seeing me as your Lakshya. You shall pass all the tests. When you can see me in every living object, living being and develop compassion for all, and do not judge anyone, you must remember, you will soon merge with my Light!"

Your Beloved,
Sai Baba

Sharanagati - Complete Surrender
Lakshya - Goal

Om Sai Ram

Chapter 30

You Are Never Alone When You Belong To Sai Baba

Humans are social animals. You always need to be among other people and have an innate need to belong. That's precisely why you always need to belong to a herd. Many of you always stay stuck in realities that may not even be yours because you fear alienation. The fear of being alone will keep you in old beliefs and conditioning for many lifetimes, probably until one day you will not be okay with being there and will need to break off. The need to be a part of a family, social group, etc., makes you a people-pleasing personality who does not stand up for your truth. You allow people to be unreasonable around you, but you do not open your mouth. There is so much fear of judgment and being left alone.

People love to alienate those who speak the truth and are good with very diplomatic people. People find those with the fire of reality very different, and they begin to distance themselves from them. You fear this alienation and do not accept your own fire. Eventually, it dies down slowly, and you feel lifeless at times. But the truth is, if the fire is burning, only then can you create good things. Only then can someone stand up, speak the truth, and make things happen. Someone has to stand up against groupism, corruption, and wrongdoing. But once you take such challenging steps, there is always a possibility that you are left alone, and others in your herd may not resonate with you anymore. It requires immense courage and strength to get away from the known and enter the unknown.

That's the soul's growth–not the need to be with the herd but to follow the path of truth under the guidance of Baba. We all know the true leader will never follow the herd. He is the lion who dares to follow a new path, and the rest will follow. The only thing you must remember is that you are not alone. You have your Sadguru, Sai Baba, always by your side.

Sai says, "Who says you are alone? Even if the entire world abandons you, I will always remain by your side. Never say you are alone. If you say that, you do not consider me your own. Being different is not easy. Standing up for your truth has never been easy. Whoever abandons or belittles you doesn't know any better, so it's not about you; it's about themselves and their inner beliefs. They may not even have the courage to accept such changes in beliefs, as they may be deeply conditioned. A radical change is never accepted gracefully. You are brave enough to understand your choices. Now do not fear anything. Make sure you push your boundaries and do the needful. I am your strength and your shield. I am your friend who will talk to you and be with you. So do not think you will be left alone; keep chanting: I am not alone; I always have Baba Sai with me. And you will feel my presence with you. Your Sai is forever tied to your soul. He never leaves any of his children alone. The Light in you must not die. You have come to break some patterns in your soul and also of the collective consciousness of your tribe. Make sure you achieve your goals. You may have thoughts of giving up. You may feel you are not thinking correctly, as all others seem to think similar to each other. You may doubt yourself and think you are wrong. In fact, they are in fear and blindfolded from seeing the truth. Your abilities to stand out have gotten you here. Stick to it, and you will see the Light soon. This dark tunnel will end. I wait on the other side of this tunnel. It's your duty to cross this tunnel with complete faith in me."

Yours Beloved,
Sai Baba

Chapter 31

The Path Of Bhakti To Baba

Shree Ram had taught nine steps of bhakti to Shabri when he visited her Kutiya. We have tried and explained 11 ways to be a true devotee of Sai.

1. A bhakta must keep company with the holy men as they are pure in thought, word, and deed, so one can remain focused on the bhakti at all times diverting the mind from worldly attractions (Jaisi sangat waisi rangat).

2. A true bhakta must hear the divine attributes of the Baba so they are fixed in the mind. Listen to his Artis or keep reading the Sai Satcharitra so the focus is on what he teaches.

3. A child of Sai must give up egoism in all its ramifications. Anything that can allow the ego to rear its head must be sacrificed or given away on the path to bhakti.

4. Guru seva is the highest service a Sai bhakt renders to the teacher. It will make him humble and capable of absorbing more knowledge and see Baba in all.

5. Singing the glories of Baba with a pure mind. It's very important to do this if one wants to get rid of past karmas and move ahead to moksha.

6. A Sai child has to develop a deep faith in Sai Baba, and nirantar japa, i.e., continuous chanting must be observed. It's one of the

most efficacious ways of realizing God. His name has so much potent power that it will automatically lead to bhakti.

7. A bhakta requires developing control over the senses, which will lead to great character. A great character is formed when the indiryas (senses). that take you to the lower desires are kept in check and your attention is directed to the divine light of Sai Baba.

8. The most important aspect is to see the whole world as pervaded with the Lord, and serving the world by giving up all maan-abhimaan (all types of ego) is equally important. It will lead to greater devotion.

9. A Bhakta must have contentment and an innocent mind–that is, a mind that cannot find faults as it sees everything as God. It sees the good in all. It sees everything as positive and auspicious. Only then can the stability of dhyana of the Lord be maintained.

10. Baba has always emphasized simplicity and straightforward behavior. He has shown by his own way of living that one should be spontaneous and natural in one's behavior. There must be no cunning quality in the devotee. His heart must be filled with humility and devotion at all times.

11. A bhakta also must render his service to Baba's devotees. It's very important because Baba's devotees carry his bhav (a strand of energy) in them. So serving them is equal to pleasing Baba.

Sai says, "I am pleased if you perform your duties well. I become very happy when I see you walking the path of a Bhakta yogi. It's one of the paths to renunciation and finally reaching me. It's the way to achieve moksha. Shedding ego is one of the most important aspects of a human's life. The more you submerge yourself in bhakti, the more you shed layers of ego. The path of sewa and bhakti will lead you to the Lord. Parvardigar is always happy when his children are on the path of truth, honesty, humility, and unconditional love. Your character will be tested by life. It will go through various paths of fire. The more tests you pass, the faster you redeem your karma and merge with me. The senses need to be controlled. Discipline in bhakti is very important. Have you seen how religiously they perform their duties in my temple every day, in and out, with the same duties? Keep your vision focused on me. I will take care of the rest of your life. Becoming an ardent devotee is a task, and it cannot be attained in one go. You have to pass severe tests of faith and surrender. That's why my two keywords, Shraddha (faith) and Saburi (patience), are very important to embody. Shed your ego and personality to be my child. Recognise my children when you meet one, as he will also carry a strand of my energy. Serving him will be serving me. I am for you and with you. No one can come between us. I love you a lot more than you love me. I love you, my child.

Yours Beloved,
Sai Baba

Kutiya - Hut

Chapter 32

Listening To Sai's Arti

Strange, isn't it, that Baba, in his living years, instructed how to perform his Artis and the protocol for the entire day? It's difficult for the human mind to understand why he would do such a thing. But it was one of his Leelas. When Saints do certain acts, our human mind may not be able to perceive the reason behind them. They are able to see the subtle energies and distant visions that our normal eyes cannot reach.

Baba had come to Earth to help humankind evolve and get rid of their karmas. He helps to ease out problems so life can progress with ease. Do not take him for granted and keep wishing without any responsibility. Baba created a whole day Arti program to help the human mind. For individuals who struggle to calm their racing thoughts or battle suicidal ideation, by listening to the Artis four times a day, a gradual shift will occur in their minds towards surrendering to Baba. Praying to Baba will relieve him of his karmic baggage. The mind that has turned negative and is spiraling down will be able to pick up its pace and move on to better positive thinking. It's miraculous when that happens.

These saints could see further than what even the psychologist might not be able to handle. Listening to the words, the vibrations will help the negative and suicidal thoughts, that are spiralling you down to clearly focus on Baba's Arti. All the worries and negative thoughts and emotions slowly disappear if you begin to hear it every single day four times a day.

The Artis are designed for praising the Lord and surrender to him, so you can gradually learn to follow the path Baba has set for you. It's a way to keep the mind, that's like a horse and takes you everywhere when not in control, in check.

Om Sai Ram

Sai says, "My Artis are for your benefit. You do not sing me praises, rather you do yourself a favor by diverting your mind from these low emotions and thoughts that do you no good. In this way, your mind and body will be immersed in faith and gratitude. You develop humility as it's a reminder that nothing belongs to you. You come from dust and go back to dust. The meaning of the word Arti is the removal of the ratri (darkness). It's also known as maha niranjana. In the traditional Arti ceremony, the flower represents the Earth (solidity), the water and accompanying handkerchief correspond with the water element (liquidity), the ghee or oil lamp represents the fire component (heat), the peacock fan conveys the precious quality of air (movement), and the yak-tail fan represents the subtle form of ether (space). The incense represents a purified state of mind and one's "intelligence" is offered through adherence to rules of timing and order of offerings. Thus, one's entire existence and all facets of material creation are symbolically offered to the Lord via the Arti ceremony. In short, you offer yourself to me every time you hear it. So the "I" becomes less in you and you are filled with my essence. The hymns, the words, and the music are all created by me and I have composed them all in a way that you will forget your worries and will be focused only on me. I am your giver and I am your protector. I will set you free. I have the power to hold you through your problems. Just follow my words and focus on my name. I am always around you and will never leave you alone."

Yours Beloved,
Sai Baba.

Nirantar japa - continous chanting
Indriya - senses
Maan Abhimaan- all types of ego
Dhyana - focus
Bhav - emotions
Bhakta yoga - path of devotion

Chapter 33

Align Your Will With The Will Of Sai

A human is constantly evolving from darkness to light. He raises his consciousness and evolves throughout his lifetime. That's the purpose of human birth–to evolve. God creates veils of illusion around you depending on your soul structure and keeps you in Maya. He throws you into different desires and gameplay and plays his Leela with you in the form of difficult experiences and challenges, so you emerge stronger and wiser.

How long it takes you to learn these lessons depends on how much you learn to surrender. It depends on how fast you learn. It depends on how you walk through the fire and face the storm. Everything is dependent on your free will, choices you make, and how you respond in a particular situation. But have you noticed that you think you control life and try to control people, situations, and experiences? But really, are you controlling? If the Lord doesn't Will it, you cannot even raise your little finger, let alone control any action.

One day you begin to realize that you are not the doer and that you only act in accordance with what's given to you. The only thing that's in your hands is to learn, observe, grow, love, and then return to the source where we came from. But sadly, most of you get lost in this maze of Maya. You cannot find your way out of the labyrinth and think that's what you are meant to do here. But being stuck within the labyrinth makes you angry, sad, and disillusioned about life. You begin to think negatively and fall into the trap of darkness. Your goal must be to rise higher and trust the will of God as your will. You need to surrender to your higher purpose.

The Awakened Sai Within You

When you learn to align your will with mine, you will feel the peace you seek. When you give up your desires for the highest good of all, you shall be redeemed from all the darkness that surrounds you. The darkness is not your foe; it's there to teach you to be light. When the light within your heart is touched and your soul lightens up, you will no longer run after mundane desires. Reveal your inner darkness to the light, and it will be burned with full intensity to cleanse your soul. But for that, you must be ready to acknowledge your darkness and know it is showing up to be released. Nothing can harm you and your family until I am there around you, always protecting you all. Release the resistance, which is a part of the illusion, and make way for the truth to descend in your crown so you can be in sync with me. I am your lighthouse. Your light will merge with mine, and we both will become one. Every time you spiral down, you need to remember to rise quickly; do not stay in darkness for too long. Only when you can lay your hand in my hand fully and let go of the need to control your life, will you begin to understand how I help you flow in your life effortlessly and seamlessly. When my will becomes your will, your life will be truly enriched and gifted. Your mind is the trickster that will keep tricking you along the way and diverting you into fear which will lead you back into control. Overcome the illusions of your mind and see me as your master. I will help you redeem your karma and set you free. Allah Malik!!"

Yours Beloved,
Sai Baba

Chapter 34

When We Put Dakshina In Sai Temple

There are many stories in Sai Satcharitra where Baba himself asks for Dakshina, or sometimes a particular amount. We have also read about how he distributed these collections to the needy and for the development of the temples, etc., around the village. It's very important to understand why you go to a temple and need to put in Dakshina.

By offering some money, you are not doing anyone else a favor. You are clearing your own karmic account, either with Baba or with your own past baggage. Baba understands the cosmic rules and knows who owes whom, what, and how much. He is your sole protector. When you deposit money in his temple, you clear your own loans, and that money, when used for others, makes good karma. It's all Baba's Leela to make you debt-free from many past burdens and create an easy flow of abundance for you. We are living in a world of duality, where giving and receiving go hand in hand and every action must have a reaction.

Every positive has a negative side, just like the two sides of a coin in this earthly realm where duality exists. When you enter a holy place to absorb the positive energy and pray, there must also be an exchange; as you have received, you must also give. By offering some money, you have made an exchange for the energy received. Baba plays such Leelas. He organized his temples, Artis and the way things must be after he is gone. He had a valid reason for everything he did. Some things may not make sense, but we should trust Baba and his ways, and do what needs to be done.

It's very important to remain humble and detached from money. Donations in the name of God also help you redeem your karma. You become even with your receiving by giving.

Sai says, "Many of you have blamed me for being greedy and asking for Dakshina. I do not take it to heart as I know your limited mind doesn't allow you to see things beyond a particular limit. My Parvardigar commands me to take money from you, and I do that to help you with your past debts. You have created so much karma with money. When you deposit money in the temples, you also clear your greed quotient and learn to give from an unconditional heart. It will help you gain more prosperity and abundance. When you take sankalp and offer me what you have promised, then your desires are truly fulfilled. It means that you offer from your heart, intending to say, "Oh, Lord, what is yours, I offer back to you." "Tera tujko arpan kya laage mera!" As a form of gratitude, it's important to return a portion back to the universe of what you have received. It also helps shed the subtle ego and helps you understand that you are not the doer. Your Parvardigar is the doer! Offer money when you come to me next, your wishes will come true. Don't do it out of greed for your desires to be fulfilled; do it from an unconditional space. You will always celebrate happiness minus your ego in the most subtle way. Your abundance is also my responsibility; I make sure that by the end of the day, you have food on your table and all your needs are met. When your heart is open to giving and receiving in equal measures without any greed or ill feelings about anyone, you will receive 'barkat', and that's my promise to you."

Yours Beloved,
Sai Baba

Dakshina - Offering Of Money To God
Barkat - Abundance

Om Sai Ram

Chapter 35

Lessons That Are Not Learnt

Many times patterns repeat in our lives. Relationships, money, careers, and even our houses have patterns. You might divorce a person but your next spouse may have lesser but similar patterns. Sometimes you have a pattern in your jobs or the way money comes and goes. It only means that lessons are still not learned.

Once you begin to learn the patterns, these challenges begin to end. So many of you are not interested in self-work. You feel that if you pray to Sai, your work will be done or your patterns will end on their own. But Sai cannot intervene in your lessons! He can guide you and show you the path, but you have to learn your lessons for sure. If you do not learn, he guides you like a stern master. The blows get harder, and it will eventually lead you to see it in its face.

Be in a space of acceptance, introspection, and deep contemplation. Only and only awareness can make you free. One needs a higher mind and a higher heart to function as a visionary for oneself. Your deep knowledge is of no use if you do not imbibe it in daily practice. Make sure you focus on self and work on it instead of just praying and expecting miracles. You will be running around in circles and achieving no results. It's like you are shown signs and messages by Sai to follow a certain path or to change some patterns within yourself but you just wait for some magic or miracle to happen. An opportunity to transform is a miracle in itself.

The real miracle is in recognising the messages, following the path, and walking the road to your goals while holding the hands of Sai. Once you begin to learn the lessons and understand why certain things occur in your life and what they mirror, you will achieve a lot of success. Sai stands tall as your guide through this process called Life.

Sai says, "I am here to take care of you and guide you. I constantly watch over you and make sure you are safe. You come with a lot of karma from the past. You carry many patterns in your soul structure, which can be positive or negative. You need to become aware of your vices and begin to change them for the better. You pray to me that you want your desires to be fulfilled, but everything can happen if you clear your karma. I take over much of your karmic baggage when you take my name or read Sai Satcharitra. But there are certain things you will need to complete yourself in your life's journey. I can hold your hand through the process. I can be your tough master. I can smoothen the roads, but you will need to walk the path. There will be no other way. You must then pray for strength and courage to do it. You must pray for clarity to see the truth. You must know that only when the changes within you occur can your external environment change. You will need to see signs from me, decode my messages, have back ups, take support but complete your work. anything you leave incomplete, you will need to carry forward to your next lifetime. Keep chanting my name, and the wisdom that you require to walk your soul path will be downloaded by me to you. You shall see miracles in your life and transcend the lower mind to your higher mind. Follow me. Pray to me always. I am forever at your service. Your Sai will lead you across the seas and make you reach the shores."

Yours Beloved,
Sai Baba.

Chapter 36

Good People Die Early

It's often heard that "God takes away good people when they are needed on Earth but doesn't take away bad people". We have also heard, "God also doesn't want bad people up there, or God needs good people up there so they are taken away faster." Haven't you heard it many times?

Let's now understand what really happens. A good person is a light body who has managed to clear his or her karma to a great extent, and when their time comes, they are able to transcend faster as they can easily move upward. We can give a synonym of a balloon, which is just filled with air so it rises up faster. Similarly, a person with negative emotions and dark energies, whose aura is dark and dense, cannot rise up to the other world gracefully as they are too heavy with these blockages. They are similar to stones, which are so heavy that they can only drown downwards more into the paatal loka (underworld) and create more suffering for them as they cannot get moksha until they deal with a sufficient amount of darkness to leave this Earth.

It's very important to keep chanting Sai's name and reading Sai Satcharitra, and not only that, but it's also very important to shed lower energies like anger, jealousy, etc. and become light on their karma. Their karmic bodies create diseases for them, which they need to shed here on Earth and have no place in God's abode. The more pure you are, the easier it is to ascend to the afterlife. Spiritual discipline is important in your daily life as it supplies you with soul food to embark on the journey to moksha.

The Awakened Sai Within You

Sai says, "I am always watching you. If you just take my name superficially and are not involved in clearing your soul and karmic body, even I cannot do much. If you refrain from wanting to take my name and attach to this material world, which is only Maya (illusion) and your samskaras (conditioning) are not good and haven't changed with time, then even the Parvardigar (God) rejects you. Your body is just a temple for your soul; use it to its fullest to help your soul create enough good karmas, wisdom, intellect, and Riddhi-Siddhi, as this human life is very precious. Take care of your body and keep it healthy so you can achieve your goals. Your need to be present in this world to just enjoy the benefits will only bring you more suffering. Do not crave things that bring you temporary happiness. Crave healing your mind, body, and soul. Crave merging with me. Crave the Light because, at the end of your life's journey, only your good karma and the light will be needed to take you across. If you haven't collected enough light through chanting and other mediums, then how will you climb the ladder to heaven? You will need it to move on. Eventually, even your body and senses will leave you. Then all you will need is me. So focus only on me and my name, and I will take you with me when the time comes. I am always waiting for my children to raise their arms to pray and ask for help from me. It fills my heart with joy when I see my children follow the path of enlightenment."

Yours Beloved,
Sai Baba.

Pataal Loka - The World Underground

Chapter 37

Manifestation Vs. Surrender

We often get confused about whether we should manifest things or live in surrender. There is a difference in both. The new age teachings teach you how to manifest your heart's desire. It teaches you how your mind is everything, and every block comes from the subconscious mind. By working on building a new neuro pathway in your brain, you create a new reality for yourself, and your heart's desires begin to fulfill themselves. But even manifestation is not complete without surrender.

They do teach you to manifest and forget about it. You will receive it in your divine time. Surrender is the highest form of prayer. Your mind might desire or want to achieve many things that may not be in alignment with your soul path. Or it may not be in your favor eventually. Your mind is a limited entity. It cannot perceive the larger picture. It's the Sadguru who can see what's good for you and what's not.

Wanting, desiring, praying and manifesting are fine provided you learn to surrender in the end. Only when your will is aligned with the will of Sai Baba, can it actually manifest in your life. Even if it's not written in your destiny, it can still be achieved by Sadguru's grace. "MAINU PATA HAI SAI, BADAL TU SAKDA HAI MERI HAATH DI LAKEERAAN." He has the power to do so; he can change your destiny and give you what's not written in your blueprint. Manifestation can come out of ego but surrender can only come out of humility. Manifestation is never complete without gratitude and surrender.

The Awakened Sai Within You

Sai says, "If a child asks for chocolate I cannot always give in to his whims and fancies. You may desire many things, but everything might not be in favor of your growth. Many times, you get stuck in the illusion of comparison and want what the other person has. You begin to run after things that may not even be meant for you. This is because your mind is full of fears, anxieties, lack, low self-esteem, and low self-belief. Always remember that each person has his own destiny. You have to believe in your own uniqueness. You do not understand and value your life's blueprint; it's for a reason that your destiny is the way it is, whether you like it or not. To get your heart's desire, first learn to accept your life as it is. Then strive for what you want. Comparing your journey with others will only bring you grief. Ask yourself: after a few years will it be worth it? If yes, then pray and manifest. Remember to be humble and in gratitude. I am always by your side. Many times I answer your prayers, which may be delayed but fulfilled. Many times you keep praying, but your wish isn't granted because I know it's not good for you in the long run. Learn to say, "Baba, if you give me this, it is good, but if you can't give me this, it is very good, and I understand that it wasn't meant for me." Only then can you stay happy and in true samarpan. "Main hoon na, dekhta jaa tere Sai ka chamatkar. Sabka bhala ho!"

Yours Beloved,
Sai Baba

Samarpan- Surrender

Chapter 38

Jaako Raakhe Saiyaan, Maar Sake Na Koi!

It's a well known quote: "Laakh bura chahe, wahi hota hai, jo manjoore khuda hota hai." Even if someone tries to cast an evil eye on you or performs any kind of black magic on you, if you are under the protection of Sai, there is nothing that can harm you. There are ample examples of how Sai has created protective shields around us. There are various ways to do it. Chanting his name, applying vibhuti, eating his prasad, visiting Shirdi, and reading Sai Satcharitra are all various ways to ensure he casts a shield on you and protects you from all harm and ill-karma.

If some mishap happens and a life is gone, then you hear everyone saying, "Nazar lag gayi." It's a well-known fact that other people's thoughts and intentions affect our lives in ways you cannot even imagine. If your aura is sensitive and easily absorbs energies, you will catch evil's eye very quickly. Some people catch it more quickly than others. You cannot stay hidden or live a life full of blocks just because there is jealousy or negativity around you. It gets very demotivating to live a life full of challenges. It creates trauma and causes ill health in the long run.

Sai will create a protective shield around your aura, and then everything negative will deflect back. It's important to perform a routine prayer to Sai so all calamities are dissolved. If you are authentic and work hard from your soul, then no evil eye can stop you from progressing. There might be delays and slow growth, but one will surely progress with Baba's shield. He will hold your hand, lead you across the storm, and ensure you are safe. You might receive blows, but you will not fall. And there will come a time when it will surely be so powerful that you will look back and realize how Sai protected you through all the calamities

Sai says: "Your bhakti is your shield. I am forever watching you. I emphasize reading my Sai Satcharitra or applying vibhuti for the same reason. It will protect you from all dangers and keep you safe. My name is your kawach. If anyone casts an eye on you, my child, I will watch him and destroy anything that's cast on you. If you feel that you have caught nazar, then come to my temple, sit for a while, and visualize all ill effects leaving your body. See it all going into the floor into the center of mother Earth, and, my child, believe me, you will feel lighter immediately. Apply my vibhuti and feel yourself becoming stronger and more energetic. You must remember that enemies, calamities, and bad times will always come, but your shield should be strong. 'Maine teri zindagi ki dor pakde hue hai. Bus chalta jaa! Applying vibhuti on your forehead, throat, and navel every day will protect your mind, body, and soul. Even if you are in the middle of a storm, continue moving forward while chanting my name. You will soon see yourself free from the bondage of evil eye and ill-karma. Your trust in my protection must be strong and not easily wavered by any doubts. My two magic words, 'Shraddha' and 'Saburi', have to be your go-to mantra to ensure your shield is strong. The stronger your trust in me, the stronger your kawach. They both go hand in hand."

Your Beloved,
Sai Baba

Kawach - Shield

Chapter 39

You Must Cross The Bridge Of Pain To Find Love

Being heartbroken in love leaves a strong impact on the mind, especially if it's in the tender age of teens or early twenties. You are not scared of loving again; you are scared of being heartbroken again. You are not scared of opening up and being vulnerable, but you are scared of exposing yourself to the wrong person and breaking down again. You are scared of the vulnerability you feel and the void you experience. You get scared of spending hours talking on the phone and texting someone your deepest secrets, revealing your insecurities, and letting them into your shadows, and they disappear or leave as if they never knew you. Slowly, you learn to protect yourself and guard your heart, because that way, you don't have to feel that kind of pain ever again. You finally decide to end the story before even writing it, even if it means missing out on what could be your happily ever after.

It's strange, but true. The fear of loving again is immense, and the majority of you do not experience love again. If love knocks on your door, you fear opening the doors of your heart. Remember one thing: the bridge to love is through pain. Each experience of love you have reflects your own inner psyche, fears, and inner demons. Until you learn to recognise them and break your past patterns, history will keep repeating itself.

There is a lot to learn and understand about love relationships. Anyone who makes you believe they are happy and all is well in their relationship is masking it. Every relationship has its payback. Every relationship needs to go to the next level, and it struggles to squeeze out of the lower level to move, or else it gets stagnated. No breakups are all of a sudden. Every breakup has its seeds planted way back, and many red flags are ignored; maybe that's why it seems sudden.

Sai says, "I am forever watching your relationships. If you worry and say, "Baba, why did you make me suffer in a marriage or an affair?" My dear one, it's very important to grow, and these experiences are your karma. I hold your space while you are experiencing it. There is no love without pain in this world of duality. The pain comes to take you out of your comfort zone. Until we walk the path of heartbreak, we won't find love. To find love, you must cross the bridge of pain. Love and pain go hand in hand. There are no wrong relationships, as everything is a learning experience since they make you stronger. You should dive more into self-love. People will come and go. They will love you and become strangers again. That's the beauty of relationships. It's how you perceive it. Love, in the end, is only from me. It's always between you and me. People who come into your life to love you are just my channels. Once their role is over, they leave. The forever love story is a myth. Have you seen how water gets stagnant when stilled? If you keep throwing stones into the water, you create ripples, but what happens then? The dirt comes up and flows away. The water becomes fresh. Similarly, these ripples that are created just separate your 'vish from the amruta' within your consciousness. That's the higher purpose. Your Sai remains constant in your life; everything else will come and go.

Yours Beloved,
Sai Baba

Om Sai Ram

Chapter 40

Life Is Enriched With Gratitude

You may feel bogged down by the challenges you face in daily life. You may feel as if life is a burden that always throws problems and hurdles at you. You may curse your life and compare your life with others. You may feel as if you are the unfortunate one, God doesn't love you, and you are abandoned by him. You will feel like you are unlucky and feel lonely. Nothing seems to work in your favor.

People around you seem blessed; they get everything on a platter, and things seem to be going well for them. They seem to be enjoying life. But there are no favorites of God. For him, each and every human is equal. He doesn't differentiate between anyone. Neither does he compare or trouble one more than the other. Everything that's happening in your life is as per your karma.

In fact, he helps you and guides you through the process. Your own actions are your creation. What are you focusing on? Are you being the victim of life and constantly crying, complaining, or brooding away? Instead of constantly focusing on the comparison and feeling belittled, you can choose to focus on the support you get amidst the drama or the help and guidance you receive. What you focus on is exactly what you will attract, as life is your own mirror. Your life is unique to your soul structure, and what you experience around you is a reality created by your own karma.

Maybe some paths will open up to resolve your challenges. When you feel gratitude for the good, even though the ratio of good might be less than the challenges, it will begin to grow. The reasons to feel gratitude will increase, and life will eventually reach a smooth balance.

The Awakened Sai Within You

Sai says, "Main tere saath hoon humesha, dukh mein aur sukh mein. I will never abandon you. I stay by your side in your happiness and your sadness. You face challenges as your soul has come to learn many lessons that will make you stronger. As you clear your karma, your soul becomes lighter and lighter, and it begins to ascend. Everything is divine play and happening perfectly as it's meant to be. When you understand that, half your problems will be solved just like that. Rest half, just follow my guidance, and you shall see how your Sai stays by your side and blesses you. Focus on your mind and thoughts that are repetitive in your head, for they will give you a clue to your internal mind mapping. That's where you will get the power to change your life. The changes in your thoughts, when they are directed more into my prayers, will make you humble and compassionate. They will lead you to live life more authentically. This will raise your life to a higher vibration. Stop complaining and judging self and others, and instantly, you will see relief in your situation. Move on from being a victim of life to an empowered child of Sai. Running from door to door will not give you relief. Sitting in silence and communicating with me will change your life forever. bringing in Gratitude before you make a wish will raise your vibrations to a higher frequency to manifest your prayers quickly. Make sure you stay in a high frequency in comparison to worry and stress. Your communication with me gets better."

Yours Beloved,
Sai Baba

Chapter 41

This Too Shall Pass

When good times don't last long, then bad times also don't last very long. It's a matter of time before things come to an end. When you are going through tough times, keep chanting this mantra: "This too shall pass". It will keep you going through the hard times and bring in a fresh ray of hope. In the moment of distress, when your grounds are shaking, Sai sends people to help you. He will never leave you alone. Recognising that help and taking it is what is required. Be open to recognising and receiving the help that comes your way.

You must know that everything is transient and nothing is permanent. Change is happening at all levels and at all times. As nothing is permanent, it applies to good times and bad times. We live in a world built on duality. It's a world where good and bad coexist together. If you experience heat, you will also experience cold. If you experience day, you will also experience night. So hold on and allow that moment to pass.

It's always important to share your problems with Sai. He looks after you like no one else does. Always look back and remember the times when they were bad and you overcame those challenges. So, this too shall pass. If you can retain your faith in such tough times and are able to see the positive even in bad times, you have achieved a high level of ascension. Your center will begin to remain balanced, and you will not shake as you used to do earlier. Your core strength will stand strong like a rock. Then you will know that your learning is done. Baba always protects and stabilizes you. And the graph of good times and bad times won't go as deep as before. You will quickly revive and center yourself.

Om Sai Ram

Sai says, "Why do you fear when I am with you? My eyes are on you 24 hours a day, 7 days a week. I am constantly watching you and taking care of you in all your bad times. I require you to be patient and keep your ears wide open. Only when you stop crying and do not panic will your mind work to acknowledge my presence and hear my guidance. Many times, I knock hard. I will come through words from another man. But you disregard those, at times, in your anger, thinking it's just empty advice—good, bad, right, wrong—all will happen. It's a part of life. The moment you think you want only good and cannot accept the bad in your life, then you operate from the ego. If you can keep your ego aside and understand that good and bad are two sides of the same coin, then you will not be perplexed by things when they go wrong. You will maintain your balance by maintaining your trust in me, and will tide smoothly through bad times. Seek my guidance and advice from time to time. I am showing you the road that will lead to your destiny. Like I have said before, everything is transient. Your Sai is the only constant in your life. When your eyes will recognise my sight and your ears will listen to my advice, then I shall exist in your heart, and then nothing can shake you or break you. Remember, I am your eternal father."

Yours Beloved,
Sai Baba

Chapter 42

Forgive Yourself and Others

Forgiveness is the highest form of good karma you can create. When you can truly forgive your abuser and see them as someone lost in their own darkness, you will develop compassion, and your higher heart will begin to open up to Divine Love. Then you are an Ansh (part) of the same God you pray to. You would have achieved the highest quality of a living soul's embodiment. And never forget to forgive self. You may not have realized how you hold yourself responsible for many things that you were ignorant about. Your inner child might be angry at you for not standing up at times when you really needed to.

You always gave in to society, your parents, in-laws, and loved ones. You sacrificed yourself and made your existence feel insignificant. You might have been holding on to that for ages in your subconscious mind. It's important to let go of toxic shame and forgive yourself. Holding on to anger for others and saying things like, "I can never forgive them for what they did to me", you not only dishonor yourself but you also dishonor Sai Baba. As a child of Sai, who loves you so much, you must know you are very precious. You must know that he would not want you to suffer.

If you keep praying for a change in the situation but haven't worked on forgiveness, even Sai will become helpless to help you. You will become empowered the moment you forgive yourself and others. When you truly leave the past behind and let go of the entire trauma, when you can tell your story without any emotional charge to it, you will have truly achieved forgiveness. When you can freely turn the chapters of your life and open a new beginning you will truly be Baba's child.

Sai says, "When Parvardigar (God) takes care of everything and nothing can move without his permission, who are you to seek revenge or stay angry at someone? Wasn't I ridiculed or abused? Did you ever see me getting angry at that person? I stood with my power and my faith in my Father above. And they got distanced on their own. So who are you to claim any revenge? Wait for the Lord to do what needs to be done. If you are true, justice will be served. Holding malice or anger against anyone will serve you no good. When you feel angry at someone, surrender them to me and let me handle it. Say, "Sai, forgive them, for they do not know what they do." It's important to understand that people come from darkness and ignorance; they may sometimes not realize what they are doing. Forgiveness doesn't free them; it frees you. Free yourself now. Make yourself light by emptying your heart into my jholi. I love you to the core, and you must remember that. Your Sai forgives you, and so you must forgive yourself. You may not be aware many times that you need to forgive yourself. Dive deep into your heart, and you will be surprised to see how much baggage you are carrying within you. It will be there in no time, as you will discard the veils of illusion and begin to see the magic and miracles in your life. You will see how life will begin to flow and how the stars will be in your favor."

Yours Beloved,
Sai Baba

Chapter 43

Fear Vs. Faith

An autonomous nervous system is made to respond in two ways: fight or flight. When the brain perceives danger, it sends signals to the body, and we react with fight or flight. In every situation, these must be overcome to form a strong balance so the situation can be perceived and worked upon. Whenever a dangerous situation arrives, one must remember Sai.

Your faith quotient should exceed your fear quotient. Do not allow fear to overpower your mind. Instead, raise your arms and say, "Sai, my father, help me. Sai, show me signs to keep the faith." It's always important to keep asking. You will receive it when you ask. The only thing that can calm down the nervous system is to know that you are safe and that can only happen when in most adverse situations, you keep your faith intact.

When you make a decision and then rely completely on Sai, he knows what is best for you. Keep repeating like a mantra, "I am safe with Sai." When you say these words, they help you stabilize and improve your body signals and bring clarity to your mind. It's only in these moments that your faith will be tested, and it's only faith that will rescue you from such moments with ease.

Faith will help you stay in good health longer than someone without any or less faith. Every fear can be overcome with faith in Sai. Make sure you understand the correlation between the two. Instead of fight or flight or freeze just replace with Faith. The more the faith, the lesser the fear. There can be no place for fear when faith exists.

The Awakened Sai Within You

In this physical dimension, the illusions create fear within you, and you respond from an unconscious space. If you will surrender to me and have faith in me, you will be able to look through the illusions of fear and learn to operate from complete and immovable faith. I am always standing by your side. If you ever feel that you are engulfed by fear, look into my eyes in my picture, and you will become fearless. Know that your Sai is with you. Just chant my name and all darkness will be dispelled. You know the use of magic words: 'OM SAI RAM'. I have created it for your benefit. Use it with utmost faith. Trust me with all outcomes, and it will work in your favor. Humans have a survival instinct. During all major calamities, your intent naturally propels you towards survival. But when you are with me, you will glide smoothly through the process as I carry you in my arms and take you across the realms. If you feel you cannot see me, then focus on your breathing, and you will eventually calm down. You will clear your fears to see me. I will not leave your side. My consciousness is merged with your consciousness, so I feel all you feel. If you fear, it only shows your faith is not stable. Clear your fear, and focus only on the faith; then it will not suffer your maximum karma. I rectify your karma and take it on me. I shall hold you tight in my arms day and night. Just keep building your faith stronger and stronger. You are the blessed child of Sai. You shall forever be under my sharan (protection).

Yours Beloved,
Sai Baba

Chapter 44

No One Loves Me

There are so many of you who may feel that no one loves you at some point. Some of you may have lost your parents at a young age or may not have parents who support you. You may even be abused by your parents, in-laws, spouse, relatives, neighbors, friends, or colleagues. You might have, at some point, felt alienated and found yourself fighting your battles alone. There are times when you might feel completely alone. You might want to pick up the phone and just pour your heart out to someone, but you may feel there is no one who is genuine enough or with whom you can be comfortable being vulnerable.

It's like you are living a life that might not feel like yours. You might feel like a misfit. You may be constantly rejected in love and crave a life partner, but nothing seems to be working. At such times, it's only Baba who holds your hand the entire time. He shows you his love and constant care in many different ways. He will never leave your side, not even for a second. You must bow down to the Sharan of Baba and know that he loves you unconditionally. He is always showering love on you.

Having no support shows your inability to trust people, which may arise from your past experiences. When you can understand that your trust in Sai will bring in the right people who can support you positively, you will be able to open your arms to people who will be sent by Sai. It will feel like you have met your soul family. It is now time to put the past aside and allow the new rays to enter your life.

The Awakened Sai Within You

Sai says, "When you attract loneliness and a lack of support, it only reflects your own beliefs. It shows your lack of faith in Sai. Beta (child), I am your eternal father. I hold your space. Talk to me like you would talk to your father or mother. Why do you not look at me when you want support? You just feel lonely and stay in that gloominess all by yourself. Do not do that to yourself! I am here. Tell me everything; I am listening to you patiently. You will feel heard by me. I will never abandon you. Sit on my lap when you want to feel loved. I will give you all the love you require; I will pat you and put you to sleep if you do not get sleep at night. Just call out to me. If you are scared of someone, ask me to help you. I am waiting for you to call me, as I cannot intervene with your free will. If you want to cry your heart out, come to my temple and sit and cry your heart out; your Baba is here to console you. I am your Father, Mother, Child, Friend, Teacher, Guide, and anything and everything you can think of. I take on different roles to make you feel loved, wanted, and heard. This world may betray you, cheat you, abandon you, or laugh at you, but your Baba won't. I will help you empower yourself to face the world in a better way. I will caress your wounds and seal them, so you are whole and complete again. I do everything to bring a smile to your face. Your Baba is here for you forever."

Yours Beloved,
Sai Baba

Chapter 45

The Path Of Truth And Honesty

"Honesty is the pathway to heaven." It's essential to walk the path of truth and honesty. Taking Sai's name and deceiving someone is the worst crime you can do. Making huge claims that you are his favorite bhakta and then misleading your family for money is uncalled for.

Do you believe that Sai remains unaware of these actions and allows you to swiftly continue with these malevolent practices? You have a mind to believe you can get away with such deceit against yourself and others. Deceiving another human is deceiving Baba himself. Wake up before it's too late, or there will be no chance for forgiveness. Using the name of Sai for selfish motives and short-term gains is the biggest foul you can play. It creates spiritual karma, and it takes lifetimes to settle such karma. The soul must always learn to survive in truth and purity.

A conscious effort must be made, and tests must be given to turn your soul into real gold. The halo you see around the Gurus and the brightness on their faces aren't just there. They come from deep meditation and clearing the blemishes of the soul.

It requires strong perseverance and determination to make yourself elite enough to be close to Sai. He watches all your actions and will strike at the right time. Ignorance and darkness will only drown you in the murk. Beware of the consequences of your karma. The law of the universe spares no one. It's impossible to escape the redemption of your actions. It takes lifetimes of pain and suffering to overcome these pieces of baggage.

The Awakened Sai Within You

Sai says, "If you are my Bhakta, you cannot be dishonest and participate in maliceful practices. So, if you claim to be the child of Sai, be aware that I am watching you. And when I raise my lathi (stick), you will not be spared. If I am the loving, compassionate Sai maa, then I am also your Baba whose anger knows no bounds if wronged. Your action is seeded for the future. Creating heaven or hell for yourself is in your hands. No one can change that. Your koti (millions) forgiveness cannot redeem your evil deeds. Hurting, deceiving, or backstabbing someone is not okay. The Paravardigar is watching everything. Make sure you correct your actions and walk with me on the path of truth. You are the creator of your own life. Do you want quick, short-term gains or long-lasting happiness and peace? The choice is always yours. Even I cannot interfere with your free will. I wait and watch you till you complete your cycle of deceit and get the blows to begin the journey of righteousness. There is no bigger truth than the Light. Running behind this false world will hurt you in the long run. If you want to attain peace, follow the Light. The Sat Chit Anand will make you Paripoorna (whole & complete)."

Yours Beloved,
Sai Baba

Lathi - Stick
Koti - Millions
Pari Poorna - Complete
Sat Chit Anand - Truth Consciousness Bliss

Chapter 46

Ascend To Merge With Sai

You work hard to keep up with the traditions of marriage, celebrations or a death in the family. There are so many dos and don'ts. You ask and try your best to make it perfect; every ritual should ultimately happen. If you don't do the same, you will be an outcast and not treated as a part of the family. You fear judgment; you may also face criticism from people around you.

The conditioning is so significant in you and all around you that if anyone dares to change how it works, you cannot resonate with it. You feel as if your sense of belonging is threatened. It is so embedded in your beliefs and cellular DNA that even if someone cannot afford it, they will take some money on a loan and do what's required.

Why judge someone who has gone through so much and cannot catch up? They are labeled as unsuccessful people or losers. If someone tries to break the pattern or the tradition, everyone else will lecture them as to how they should not do it differently. You all are like frogs stuck in a pond. You will pull him down even if he wants to get out and achieve a different vision. Your perception is not the only perception. If that's shown to you, then you comment, "Oh, they are different from us. We do it this way."

It's a sign you are stuck in societal conditioning, which would mean your growth is also stuck. Learn to understand different possibilities and be open to change. Only changing your thoughts can break patterns coming down through generations.

Sai says, "I was the most liberal when I lived on Earth. Did I bind you to any samskaras or religions? Did I tell you to pray day and night endlessly ritualistically or follow a set way of living? I didn't follow the norms of a saint, but I showed you how to have a pure heart and soul was above all the rituals. I always taught you to be open to change and live a simple life by my own example. I showed you by living on the bare necessities and being compassionate for others, you can ascend the ladder to spiritual growth. I showed you humility and love go hand in hand. I showed you high thinking by forgiving others and clearing your karma by loving those who hate you. Let everyone follow their dreams and their paths in life. If you judge others, you will, too, be judged. If you want to change, you need to be the change. Do not ridicule others; admire their ability to do things differently. Support their cause. Stay silent and hold their space. Learn good habits from others. Share your thoughts freely and learn to listen intently. Grow and understand at all times, in every moment. Sai loves his children doing this. I will bring you closer to my heart and soul. I will embrace your being in mine. Eventually, you will become me. I will become you. Your Sai awaits your ascension, which can happen only through your own free will in accordance with your destiny. I hold your hand through it all. Sabka Maalik Ek!!"

Yours Beloved,
Sai Baba

Om Sai Ram

Chapter 47

Bhiksha

Sai Baba used to collect his food in the form of Bhiksha every day. He usually confined his 'Bhiksha' rounds to the same five houses, all within a few meters of Dwarkamai. Baba would stand outside and call for bread, but he never entered the houses. Baba collected the food in a cloth bag and any liquids in a tin mug then returned it to Dwarkamai. He would offer some at the Dhuni and empty the rest into a pot (the kolamba) by the fire, where any creature could take from it. Only later would Baba eat a small amount himself.

Now let's understand the Leela behind it. Firstly, he, as a soul, showed through this method of eating his meals how to live egoless without owning even a morsel of food. Not owning anything sheds the subtlest of the ego of a human. It also shows that you are always provided for. No matter what, God will always give us food. You can never go hungry.

Another teaching from the Gita is that you come with nothing and leave with nothing. You own nothing. Baba showed us a living example of how to live a simple life. His simplistic lifestyle and habits showed us how to live egoless and karma-free. The highest of the bhakta, like Sudama, was made to collect his food through Bhiksha so he could let go of the subtlest ego of being the biggest devotee of Krishna. Even that ego has to be shed eventually. The soul must drop everything to become free.

Apart from shedding the ego, food also creates karma like, greed and evil tendencies due to hunger. When we can live like Sai, we will have touched a great deal of our soul essence.

Sai says, "I came from the Light and went back into the Light. My origins are unknown, as I was not born and did not die. I do not need anything, as I can manifest anything I want with a twitch of my fingers. But I still chose to come in the form of a Fakir. My life was to show you how to live in a completely humble, egoless state. Begging for food dissolves all the karma you have with food. When you eat in a langar, you dissolve the karmas of many lifetimes. You remain humble and surrender to eating what you get. Your quenching and greed for good food and taste are also karma. Eating humbly from what's given to you devoid of taste will dissolve your sense of taste so you can transcend it. Have you noticed your greed for good food and liquor, your addictions to tea, chocolates, sugar, and whatnot? It's all karma. I showed you that after begging, when I cooked and shared it with others as prasad to humans, animals, and birds, I showed you that we are all one. This act opens the heart unconditionally to all. The opening of the heart awakens the higher heart, and you connect to the Paravardigar. Then the light from the Parvardigar descends on you to make your karma less. Food karma is dissolved and cleared. Follow my path. Walk in my footsteps, and the father of this universe will forgive your sins and grant you a boon to moksha."

Yours Beloved,
Sai Baba

SAI BABA WALKING IN THE VILLAGE

OM SAI RAM

Chapter 48

Always See Humor In Your Challenges

Life should be a merger of happiness and commitment. You must be responsible for all your actions, as they create karma. But you must also know that you must be light and take all things lightly. Make humor a part of your daily life, and you will not feel the burden of life pushing you down. Your attitude towards your life experiences is essential to bringing about positive changes.

How you perceive them is vital to your response to them. If you can bring humor into it, life will also lighten up and give you less challenging experiences. If you remain grumpy and angry at life, throwing in criticism, judgment, and curses, then your life will reflect the same back to you. Think of it as what you sow, so shall you receive. If something comes your way, knowing how to respond is important.

Build strength and resilience, change your mindset, and heal your inner wounds. Slowly, the negative won't even affect you. When you can laugh at it, you take your power back from it. Then the experience loses its power over you, and it will soon dissipate. Why brood over spilt milk? Life is so beautiful; focus on the beauty of life and be in sync with nature.

When you feel oneness with nature, you will begin harmonizing your life. It will sail smoothly and flow better. Improve your relationship with life with the help of your devotion and love for Sai Baba. He will help you bring joy to your life. When you have humor, you will attract a good joyful life.

The Awakened Sai Within You

Sai says, "Do not take life's experiences too seriously. Above all, do not let them hurt you, for in reality, they are nothing but dream experiences (illusions). If circumstances are wrong and you must bear them, do not make them a part of yourself. They are not you. Play your part in life, but remember that it is only a role. And you have the power to change your position at any time. What you lose in the world will not be a loss to your soul. Your soul belongs to me. I am your caretaker. Trust in your Sai and destroy fear, which paralyzes all efforts to succeed and attracts the very thing you fear. Give all your worries to me in my jholi. When you have faith in me, the worst experiences should not deter you. You must stand tall as a child of Sai and become an example for others who can look up to you and follow the path of dharma. Be a magnet for happiness and joy, and that's what you will attract. Mere bachon (my children), hold my hand and laugh all your experiences out. It's only Maya. When you laugh at Maya, she loses her power. You become stronger and attract more positive experiences.

"Chola pehna Sai balak da, kyon ghabraye tu, Sai raksha hardum karien, bus dhyan lagaye tu. Hasta jaa, yahi arth hai jeevan ka, kyun aas lagaye behta tu. Sai tere paas hai phir kyon ghabraye tu."

Yours Beloved,
Sai Baba

Chapter 49

Karma With Words

Remember never to underestimate the power of words. Words uttered are energies created in the universe and impact your life and that of others. Any words spoken in rage and intense emotions become like a vow that can create havoc in your or others' lives. Suppose you are outraged; refrain from speaking ill about others or life itself. The yoyo effect will catch you in it too. The tone of your voice and the words used to explain something are also fundamental. Foul and cuss words also create major karma. You have said it loosely and forgotten about it. Your tongue also carries karma and creates dosha.

Self-control and discipline can save you from many mishaps. If evil thoughts trouble you, taking the name of the Guru or chanting any mantra can keep you from speaking or being evil. Awareness plays a key role here, as you will not understand what wrong you are doing and how to save yourself from it. Whenever you feel like uttering a curse or a bad word, utter Sai Baba's name instead. It will release you from the bondage of foul language.

Every time you say something very harsh, it's like an arrow that's left your mouth and has reached the other person to hit them. They remember it for years, and it has an effect on their minds or lives for a long time after you have said and forgotten it. It's not good for your soul's growth. The arrows will probably remain with them their entire lives, and they will likely carry them into their next lives. If you are a parent, be careful about how you speak to your child; it may create wounds in them; If you are a child, be careful how you talk to them about; hurting them will hurt Mother and Father God. Hurting any other human being will come back to you in one way or another unless you have asked for forgiveness. Praising others and reading discourses should be more spoken than anything else.

Sai says, "Maa Saraswati sits on the tongue every day. Your words are a medium that Parvardigar has given you to communicate with other human Beings. It's a medium of expression. You must learn to respect and value it. Be an observer and understand how you communicate. Do you appear like a tyrant or a dictator? Are you so soft that people treat you very casually? Does your presence intimidate people? How do you speak when you get upset? Observe the way people respond to you. Do they walk away? Do you have the strength to apologize when you hurt people? You must also accumulate enough power to forgive people when they err. It's a sign of weakness when you are unable to let go. In your profound pain, you can curse or say harsh words, which can entangle you later. Your language, code of conduct, and lines of respect should be maintained, as you are my child and cannot show meanness. When you use foul language, you lower your vibrations, and every word holds a vibration. Make sure your choice of words is from the higher realm. The higher and purer your language is, the more blessings you will attract in your life. Talking and using words are to be done with high responsibility. Talking cuss words irresponsibly will create huge karma. If you belong to my family and want me to love you as your mother, you must abide by these norms. Your Baba is always watching you, my child. Do not let me down."

Yours Beloved,
Sai Baba

Chapter 50

Baba's Promise To Mankind!

Baba made certain promises to his children, which we all have witnessed to be true in deep gratitude.

These are some of the promises Sai Baba made to his devotees during his life. He preached the importance of the "realization of the self" and criticized "love towards perishable things". His teachings concentrate on a moral code of love, forgiveness, helping others, charity, contentment, inner peace, devotion to God, and guru. He stressed the importance of surrendering to the true Sadguru, who, having trod the path to divine consciousness, will lead the disciple through the jungle of spiritual training.

1. He, whoever worships me with unmoving devotion, I care for their wellbeing. Whoever puts his feet on Shirdi's soil, will see his suffering will come to an end.

2. The wretched and miserable would rise into plenty of joy and happiness as soon as they climb the steps of my samadhi.

3. My tomb shall bless and speak to the needs of my devotees. I shall be ever active and vigorous even after leaving this earthly body.

4. If a man utters my name with love, I will fulfill all his wishes and increase his devotion. And if he sings earnestly of my life and deeds, I will be in front of him, behind him, and on all sides.

5. It is my special characteristic to free any person who surrenders to me completely, who worships me faithfully and

who remembers me, and meditates upon me constantly, and realizes the truth.

6. If you cast your burden on me, I shall indeed bear it. There shall be no want in the house of my devotees.

7. Those devotees attached to my heart and soul will naturally feel happy when they hear these stories. If anybody sings my Leelas, I will give infinite joy and everlasting contentment.

8. I will draw out my devotees from the jaws of death. If my Leelas are listened to, all diseases will be eliminated, so hear my Leelas with respect, and think and meditate on them, and assimilate them. This is the way to happiness and contentment.

9. The ego of my devotees will vanish, the listeners' minds will be set at rest, and their faith in me will be reinforced when they become one with the supreme consciousness. The simple remembrance of my name as Sai will do away with sins of speech.

10. In whatever faith men worship me, even so, do I render it to them. He whoever surrenders his mind (in devotion), body (in service), and money (in service and as a token of sacrifice) in me will be saved by me in all troubles, no matter how big they are.

11. If you give me one rupee, I owe you ten rupees back. (Tenfold of love, devotion, and service). I take care of my devotee's sufferings and take them on to me.

श्री अनंतकोटी ब्रह्मांडनायक राजाधिराज योगिराज परब्रह्म श्री सच्चिदानंद सद्गुरु श्री साईनाथ महाराज की जय...!

Shree Ananta Koti Brahmadanayak Rajadhiraj Yogiraj Parabrahma Shri Sachinanand Sadguru Sainath Maharaj ki Jai !!

Sai says," *When I make a promise I stick by it. I am your Guru and your faith in me must be atal (always). It's not easy to stick by the faith in times of distress especially if you do not see me in human form. These promises are not just words, they are my vacchan (promises) to my devotees, that I will be present long after I am gone. Your pain is my pain. You just have to call my name and I will always be there by your side absorbing your pain. In return I ask for your surrender to me, so your limited mind doesn't interfere in my intervention. Your constant focus on me will relieve you of unnecessary negative thoughts and free you from making more karma. Singing my praises will keep you in a state of non-judgement for others. JJoy and contentment will be your partners as you build new positive memories in your brain. I have enriched the land of Shirdi in such a way that when you step into the land, you will find me there as a blessing. Visiting Shirdi will remind you of your association with me and strengthen our bond, along with increasing your faith in me. You must remember to check your ego from time to time. My children have to have a special code of conduct. When you spoil your name or behave out of greed, selfishness, or revenge, you also spoil my name, as I am also associated with you. It's imperative to have a good code of conduct, which will not only add to your good karma but will also enhance the name of all my children who are associated with me. You need to be responsible if you need grace. I am always watching you all.*"

Yours Beloved,
Sai Baba

Om Sai Ram

Prologue

My relationship with Sai Baba is special and Atoot (forever, which cannot be broken) for me. I bow my head to the Lotus feet of Baba for being with me and being the caretaker of my soul on my life's journey. I feel truly blessed to be called a child of Sai. He has cared for me as his child and ensured I crossed the oceans of my life smoothly.

I was born into a family of Sai Baba devotees. Both my parents' sides of the family are Sai Baba devotees. I was born and brought up with unquestionable faith in Sai Baba. It never occurred to me that there could be another option. With Sai Baba's grace, and I firmly believe because of him, I have also experienced the blessings and cosmic presence of Satya Sai Baba, Kamu Baba of Goregaon, Narayan Baba of Panvel, and many more reverent Gurus from time to time. I have seen the miracles of Sai Baba all my life.

"Jiska Koi Nahi Uska Sai Baba Hai" is a statement that can be felt from the heart. Not once will you feel lonely in this harsh world with Sai's hand on your head.

My first visit to Sai Baba's pavan land, Shirdi, was when I was maybe seven years old. I still remember how simple the village was back then. My entire family would go together to visit Shirdi. We would park the car right outside the temple, wash our hands and faces in the nearby tap built for that, and go for Darshan. My father used to say we must first visit Baba and then check in somewhere or eat a meal. We would have a lovely Darshan. As a child, we would go right up to the Baba statue in the temple and run around in the temple and play there while my father would read Baba's book and meditate on Sai Baba. I remember the first time we bought his statue home and placed it in our living room. We grew up in Baba's chhayaa (shadow) and would always feel his grace with us.

Om Sai Ram

When I was a child, my father taught me the mantra,
Jal Tu Jalal Tu
Sai Bemisaal Tu
Mushkil Khusha Tu
Aayi Bala Ko Taal Tu

He would explain to us to use this every time we fear the dark, worry about our results, or have some pain or injury; in short, it was a multipurpose mantra that was a remedy to all our problems.

We lived a wonderful childhood with the grace of Sai. Devotion to Baba was a default in our entire family clan. I am so proud of this fact and respect my entire soul family for it.

My hardest tests were yet to come. Once this trust and faith were set, I experienced Sai Leela in many forms. I would like to write about a few here to share the valuable life lessons I learned.

When I married, I saw that my in-laws were non-believers in Sai Baba, and I saw no remembrance or reference to him. I would feel very upset during my initial years. When I went through tough times, I would always feel as if Sai Baba had abandoned me and was punishing me for some sins of mine. I felt he had dumped me in a dark hole for some bad karma I had done.

I would cry for Baba to come to this house and reside, but in vain. With every challenge, I felt deserted by Baba. Then, in the year 2000, I lost my father, and I felt as if I was all alone in this world to fend for myself. My backing and support were completely gone. I went through the journey of the night of my soul and felt as if all was lost and I was in complete darkness.

In 2002, one day, a group of people led me to a channelling session. There I sat amidst the crowd of approximately 50 people, and no one knew me there except the one who had taken me with her. In my second session, I was called among the five of us, and we were told that Sai Baba wanted to speak to us all. When we sat on the ground there, he came through a lady (name withheld) who began to channel Sai Baba.

Sai Baba spoke through her and said, "Beta (child), you think I have deserted you, and you feel lost, but that's not so. I can never desert my children. You belong to me in all your past and present lifetimes. And you will belong to me in all your future lifetimes.

Think of me as a red rose when you want to remember me, and I shall be present always in your aid." Hearing these words as if they were coming straight from Baba's mouth, I realised he was watching me. I understood his Leela to make me stronger and instill more faith in me. I was in a trance for three days, crying and laughing simultaneously. I saw my life transform from fear to faith, from lower self to higher self, with paths opening up. I have never looked back since.

This was my first direct encounter with Baba and the miracles he performed. I soon got my beautiful oil painting frame of Baba in my house, and it's placed on a wall across the main door, where we can see him every time we enter the house. I believed he was with me every time I thought of him. I would get blocked by my stress and fears, which would stop the flow of grace. I also believe he is sakshaat on this wall, looking after my family and protecting us.

I had another beautiful experience in 2010 when I got his saakshat (direct) darshan in human form in Dwarkamai. It was the most beautiful experience that I have ever encountered. I was travelling with my family, and my friend was also with us with her family. We had both awakened fresh and were excited like small children. I remember my father always telling me that Baba still visited Dwarkamai.

He would first go to Dwarkamai when he arrived, and before leaving, he would stand there and ask Baba's permission to leave home. He would explain that Baba still lived in Dwarkamai, and many people have felt him here at night.

We, both friends, had decided to spend the entire night in Dwarkamai and see if we could meet Sai there. We spent the entire day doing the lovely Darshan of his Samadhi and all the temples. At night, after winding off dinner and putting the children to sleep, we both walked our way to Dwarkamai. It was empty at 10 p.m.; we went in and sat down facing Dwarkamai. We meditated on Baba's name and waited for him to arrive.

As the clock struck 12:00 am, the climate changed suddenly; it became freezing cold. Our teeth began to chatter. He walked into the gates of Dwarkamai and came and sat facing us. As we all know, Sai Baba was in the garb of a Fakir. He had a few broken teeth and was laughing and talking to himself. Little did our ignorant minds know that Sai loved us so much that he would actually arrive in human form and that his Leela plays the game of illusion. My friend nudged me and told me, "See, Anita, Baba has come." I failed to recognise him as I imagined someone who looked like the bright marble Murti (statue) we always associate Baba with.

My ignorant mind refused to believe it was Baba. He kept on laughing at our ignorance. My friend kept nudging me. She said, "Anita, this is Baba." I just shrugged it off, saying, "No, this cannot be Baba." It's said, "When God arrives, the human mind needs to stop existing to recognise him." Sitting in that chilly weather became very difficult, and our chattering of teeth increased. It was freezing to another level, like maybe we had reached Mount Kailasa. The Sakshat Darshan was so intoxicating that our human body couldn't bear it any longer.

We finally got up to leave. Baba was still laughing and talking to himself. I am sure he must laugh at my foolishness for calling him and yet not recognising him. It was like a parent understanding his child's ignorance and stubbornness.

We finally stood up and began to walk out of the gates of Dwarkamai. The guard there asked us, "Didi, sit down for longer; why are you leaving so early?" It was as if Baba was speaking through him. He surely knew of our plan to sit there the entire night. But alas, we were neither prepared for such encounters nor had the resources built within us to sustain them. We were like immature kids running around trying to touch the moon, and when the moon came down to us, we didn't know how to handle it.

Isn't this paradox a part of our human life?

Finally, we walked our way to the hotel and slept. We woke up in the morning and drove back to Mumbai. I slept off on the journey, and just as we were about to reach the limits of Mumbai, I was about to wake up and was in between the conscious and unconscious states. I saw a vision of someone standing with his back to me, and then he turned towards me, and I saw Baba. The same Fakir we encountered the previous night I said, "Baba?" He laughed and said, "So, who do you think it was? You asked me to come, and I came." He was still laughing at Leela. I asked him, "Baba, why are you showing me this vision and not my friend?" Sai replied, "Would you have believed her?" And he disappeared.

I sat mesmerised and in a state of overwhelm at this beautiful encounter with our Beloved Sai. He showed me he existed and listened to me and my every thought. Baba was surely omnipotent and omnipresent.

Years passed by with his grace, and I felt safe and secure with Sai Baba's love showered on me. There was another time along my life's journey when I faced challenges when Baba spoke through people and sent messages. I would hear his voice loud and clear in my ears. I would get guidance on how to go about my challenge. It was nothing less than a miracle.

I found my path and my answers. I began my journey of channeling Sai Baba, and I got to design Sai Baba's Guidance cards with his grace in 2017. He guided me with a clear vision of everything he wanted. I feel his grace on me at all times, good or bad.

The beautiful miracle of my daughter's wedding was that everyone, from the decorator to the photographer to the designer, was a child of Sai Baba. It was a beautiful journey, and it was a fairy tale wedding designed by Sai Baba himself.

He has stood by me through my toughest times like a rock, holding my hand through it all. I am led by his grace alone. He has prompted this book and every word in it. He has been sending messages for a long time, but I thought I would need to be more knowledgeable about what Baba wanted me to write. I forgot that it was not my job to think. It was his grace that enabled me to write.

I think I have managed to write what he has guided me to write. And I truly believe this book will reach everyone who is meant to read it and get his message from it. The book intends to get answers to the many unanswered questions we have about Sai. He has graced us with his love through this book. I wish healing to all who read it.

I sincerely thank all those who have helped me create this book and bring it to life. It's throbbing with the heartbeat of Baba. He is in the red rose, which we all receive occasionally. His love emanates through the words in the book. His consciousness, through this book, awakens us to enlightenment. The lighthouse will guide us across the darkness in our lives.

The Guru comes in various ways to hold our hands, and this book is one of the ways he holds your hand to help you cross the oceans of samskaras.

Om Sai Ram

THIS IS EXACTLY HOW OUR BELOVED SAI BABA CAME AND SAT WATCHING US AND LAUGHING AT OUR IGNORANCE !!

Om Sai Ram

You Write. We Publish.

To publish your own book, contact us.

We publish poetry collections, short story collections, novellas and novels.

contact@thewriteorder.com

Instagram- thewriteorder

www.facebook.com/thewriteorder

www.ingramcontent.com/pod-product-compliance
Lightning Source LLC
LaVergne TN
LVHW010338070526
838199LV00065B/5752